THE ANNOTATED SHAKESPEARE

King Lear

⚜

William Shakespeare

Edited, fully annotated, and introduced by Burton Raffel
With an essay by Harold Bloom

THE ANNOTATED SHAKESPEARE

Yale University Press · New Haven and London

Essay by Harold Bloom excerpted from Harold Bloom's Modern Critical
Interpretations, *Wiliam Shakespeare's King Lear,* copyright © 1987.

Designed by Rebecca Gibb.
Set in Bembo type by The Composing Room of Michigan, Inc.
Printed in the United States of America by R. R. Donnelley & Sons.

Library of Congress Cataloging-in-Publication Data
Shakespeare, William, 1564–1616.
King Lear / William Shakespeare ; edited, fully annotated, and introduced
by Burton Raffel ; with an essay by Harold Bloom.
p.   cm. — (The annotated Shakespeare)
Includes bibliographical references.
ISBN-13: 978-0-300-12200-8 (paperbound)
1. Lear, King (Legendary character)—Drama.   2. Inheritance and succes-
sion—Drama.   3. Fathers and daughters—Drama.   4. Kings and rulers—
Drama.   5. Aging parents—Drama.   6. Britons—Drama.   I. Raffel,
Burton.   II. Bloom, Harold.   III. Title.
PR2819.A2 B55 2007
822.3'3—dc22
2006036627

A catalogue record for this book is available from the British Library.

10 9 8 7 6 5 4 3 2 1

For Ray Authement

CONTENTS

A bandoned to a raging storm, in act 3, scene 2, Lear speaks these memorable lines:

> Let the great gods,
> That keep this dreadful pudder o'er our heads,
> Find out their enemies now. Tremble thou wretch,
> That hast within thee undivulgèd crimes,
> Unwhipped of justice. Hide thee, thou bloody hand –
> Thou perjured – and thou simular man of virtue
> That art incestuous. Caitiff, to pieces shake,
> That under covert and convenient seeming
> Hast practiced on man's life. Close pent-up guilts,
> Rive your concealing continents, and cry
> These dreadful summoners grace. I am a man
> More sinned against than sinning.

This was perfectly understandable, we must assume, to the mostly very average persons who paid to watch Elizabethan plays. But who today can make full or comfortable sense of it? In this very fully annotated edition, I therefore present this passage, not in the bare form quoted above, but thoroughly supported by bottom-of-the-page notes:

> Let the great gods,
> That keep this dreadful pudder[1] o'er our heads,
> Find out[2] their enemies now. Tremble thou wretch,
> That hast within thee undivulgèd crimes,
> Unwhipped of[3] justice. Hide thee, thou bloody hand –
> Thou perjured – and thou simular[4] man of virtue
> That art incestuous. Caitiff,[5] to pieces shake,
> That under covert and convenient seeming
> Hast practiced on man's life. Close pent-up guilts,
> Rive[6] your concealing continents,[7] and cry
> These dreadful summoners grace.[8] I am a man
> More sinned against than sinning.

Without full explanation of words that have over the years shifted in meaning, and usages that have been altered, neither the modern reader nor the modern listener is likely to be equipped for anything like full comprehension.

I believe annotations of this sort create the necessary bridges, from Shakespeare's four-centuries-old English across to ours. Some readers, to be sure, will be able to comprehend unusual, historically different meanings without any glosses. Those not fa-

---

1 pudder = turmoil, uproar
2 find out = discover
3 by
4 simulating, pretending
5 villain, wretch
6 tear apart, split, destroy
7 contents
8 cry these dreadful summoners grace = cry/beg for grace from these terrible bailiffs / arresting officers

miliar with the modern meaning of particular words will easily find clear, simple definitions in any modern dictionary. But most readers are not likely to understand Shakespeare's intended meaning, absent such glosses as I here offer.

My annotation practices have followed the same principles used in *The Annotated Milton,* published in 1999, and in my annotated editions of *Hamlet,* published (as the initial volume in this series) in 2003, *Romeo and Juliet* (published in 2004), and subsequent volumes in this series. Classroom experience has validated these editions. Classes of mixed upper-level undergraduates and graduate students have more quickly and thoroughly transcended language barriers than ever before. This allows the teacher, or a general reader without a teacher, to move more promptly and confidently to the nonlinguistic matters that have made Shakespeare and Milton great and important poets.

It is the inevitable forces of linguistic change, operant in all living tongues, which have inevitably created such wide degrees of obstacles to ready comprehension—not only sharply different meanings, but subtle, partial shifts in meaning that allow us to think we understand when, alas, we do not. Speakers of related languages like Dutch and German also experience this shifting of the linguistic ground. Like early Modern English (ca. 1600) and the Modern English now current, those languages are too close for those who know only one language, and not the other, to be readily able always to recognize what they correctly understand and what they do not. When, for example, a speaker of Dutch says, "Men kofer is kapot," a speaker of German will know that something belonging to the Dutchman is broken ("kapot" = "kaputt" in German, and "men" = "mein"). But without more linguistic awareness than the average person is apt to have, the

German speaker will not identify "kofer" ("trunk" in Dutch) with "Körper"—a modern German word meaning "physique, build, body." The closest word to "kofer" in modern German, indeed, is "Scrankkoffer," which is too large a leap for ready comprehension. Speakers of different Romance languages (French, Spanish, Italian), and all other related but not identical tongues, all experience these difficulties, as well as the difficulty of understanding a text written in their own language five, or six, or seven hundred years earlier. Shakespeare's English is not yet so old that it requires, like many historical texts in French and German, or like Old English texts—for example, *Beowulf*—a modern translation. Much poetry evaporates in translation: language is immensely particular. The sheer *sound* of Dante in thirteenth-century Italian is profoundly worth preserving. So too is the sound of Shakespeare.

I have annotated prosody (metrics) only when it seemed truly necessary or particularly helpful. Readers should have no problem with the silent "e" in past participles (loved, returned, missed). Except in the few instances where modern usage syllabifies the "e," whenever an "e" in Shakespeare is *not* silent, it is marked "è." The notation used for prosody, which is also used in the explanation of Elizabethan pronunciation, follows the extremely simple form of my *From Stress to Stress: An Autobiography of English Prosody* (see "Further Reading," near the end of this book). Syllables with metrical stress are capitalized; all other syllables are in lowercase letters. I have managed to employ normalized Elizabethan spellings, in most indications of pronunciation, but I have sometimes been obliged to deviate, in the higher interest of being understood.

I have annotated, as well, a limited number of such other matters, sometimes of interpretation, sometimes of general or historical relevance, as have seemed to me seriously worthy of inclusion. These annotations have been most carefully restricted: this is not intended to be a book of literary commentary. It is for that reason that the glossing of metaphors has been severely restricted. There is almost literally no end to discussion and/or analysis of metaphor, especially in Shakespeare. To yield to temptation might well be to double or triple the size of this book—and would also change it from a historically oriented language guide to a work of an unsteadily mixed nature. In the process, I believe, neither language nor literature would be well or clearly served.

Where it seemed useful, and not obstructive of important textual matters, I have modernized spelling, including capitalization. Spelling is not on the whole a basic issue, but punctuation and lineation must be given high respect. Neither the Quarto nor the Folio uses few exclamation marks or semicolons, which is to be sure a matter of the conventions of a very different era. Still, our modern preferences cannot be lightly substituted for what is, after a fashion, the closest thing to a Shakespeare manuscript we are likely ever to have. We do not know whether these particular seventeenth-century printers, like most of that time, were responsible for question marks, commas, periods, and, especially, all-purpose colons, or whether these particular printers tried to follow their handwritten sources. Nor do we know if those sources, or what part thereof, might have been in Shakespeare's own hand. But in spite of these equivocations and uncertainties, it remains true that, to a very considerable extent, punctuation tends to result from just how the mind responsible for that punctuating *hears* the text. And twenty-first-century minds have no business, in such matters, overruling seventeenth-century ones. Whoever the compositors were, they were more or less Shakespeare's contemporaries, and we are not.

Accordingly, when either of the original printed texts uses a comma, we are being signaled that *they* (whoever "they" were) heard the text, not coming to a syntactic stop, but continuing to some later stopping point. To replace commas with editorial periods is thus risky and on the whole an undesirable practice. (The dramatic action of a tragedy, to be sure, may require us, for twenty-first-century readers, to highlight what four-hundred-year-old punctuation standards may not make clear—and may even, at times, misrepresent.)

When the printed texts have a colon, what we are being signaled is that *they* heard a syntactic stop—though not necessarily or even usually the particular kind of syntactic stop we associate, today, with the colon. It is therefore inappropriate to substitute editorial commas for original colons. It is also inappropriate to employ editorial colons when *their* syntactic usage of colons does not match ours. In general, the closest thing to *their* syntactic sense of the colon is our (and their) period.

The printed interrogation (question) marks, too, merit extremely respectful handling. In particular, modern editorial exclamation marks should very rarely be substituted for seventeenth-century interrogation marks.

It follows from these considerations that the movement and sometimes the meaning of what we must take to be Shakespeare's play will at times be different, depending on whose punctuation we follow, *theirs* or our own. I have tried, here, to use the printed seventeenth-century texts as a guide to both *hearing* and *understanding* what Shakespeare wrote.

Since the original printed texts (there not being, as there never are for Shakespeare, any surviving manuscripts) are frequently careless as well as self-contradictory, I have been relatively free with the wording of stage directions—and in some cases have added brief directions, to indicate who is speaking to whom. I have made no emendations; I have necessarily been obliged to make choices. Textual decisions have been annotated when the differences between or among the original printed texts seem either marked or of unusual interest.

In the interests of compactness and brevity, I have employed in my annotations (as consistently as I am able) a number of stylistic and typographical devices:

- The annotation of a single word does not repeat that word

- The annotation of more than one word repeats the words being annotated, which are followed by an equals sign and then by the annotation; the footnote number in the text is placed after the last of the words being annotated

- In annotations of a single word, alternative meanings are usually separated by commas; if there are distinctly different ranges of meaning, the annotations are separated by arabic numerals inside parentheses—(1), (2), and so on; in more complexly worded annotations, alternative meanings expressed by a single word are linked by a forward slash, or solidus: /

- Explanations of textual meaning are not in parentheses; comments about textual meaning are

- Except for proper nouns, the word at the beginning of all annotations is in lower case

- Uncertainties are followed by a question mark, set in parentheses: (?)

- When particularly relevant, "translations" into twenty-first-century English have been added, in parentheses

- Annotations of repeated words are *not* repeated. Explanations of the *first* instance of such common words are followed by the sign ★. Readers may easily track down the first annotation, using the brief Finding List at the back of the book. Words with entirely separate meanings are annotated *only* for meanings no longer current in Modern English.

The most important typographical device here employed is the sign ★ placed after the first (and only) annotation of words and phrases occurring more than once. There is an alphabetically arranged listing of such words and phrases in the Finding List at the back of the book. The Finding List contains no annotations but simply gives the words or phrases themselves and the numbers of the relevant act, the scene within that act, and the foot-note number within that scene for the word's first occurrence.

INTRODUCTION

*L*ear would be an excellent choice for the most virtuosic play Shakespeare ever wrote. It has great verbal brilliance—but so too do *Hamlet, Romeo and Juliet, Twelfth Night,* and indeed others of his plays as well. Although brilliance and Shakespeare regularly walk hand in hand, A.C. Bradley begins his famous lecture on *Lear* with the following statement: "*King Lear* has again and again been described as Shakespeare's greatest work, the best of his plays, the tragedy in which he exhibits most fully his multitudinous powers." But Bradley then adds that "*King Lear* seems to me Shakespeare's greatest achievement, but it seems to me *not* his greatest play."[1]

Nor has Bradley been the only querulous critic. Jan Kott, who like Bradley loves the play, begins his discussion of *Lear* as follows: "The attitude of modern criticism to *King Lear* is ambiguous and somehow embarrassed. Doubtless *King Lear* is still recognized as a masterpiece. . . . But at the same time *King Lear* gives one the impression of a high mountain that everyone admires but no one particularly wishes to climb."[2] A dedicated theater professional, Margaret Webster, confesses that *Lear* "seems to me baffling from the very beginning." She explains: "If the dramatic structure of the play had stood, clean and firm, around [its] tempestuous center, it would still be actable; Lear himself would be upheld by it. But, in my view, he is not. . . . The practical objections which I have here outlined [omitted here] may seem picayune to the enthralled and worshipping reader, but I believe they have almost always proved fatal to the play in performance, because Shakespeare has not given us the means to resolve them, but substituted a cloak of dark magnificence which we may throw around them, hoping that no one will look beneath it."[3]

Of course, all Shakespeare's plays, early and late, are stageworthy. He was, after all, what we today would have to call a commercial playwright (though "commercial" in this context has taken on a negative connotation the Elizabethans would not have intended, had they used the word at all—and they did not). Yet is there another of his plays that features eye-popping stage effects of so wide-ranging a variety, from gutta percha eyeballs dropping onto the stage (with surely a splash of red paint to heighten audience reaction), to bravura emotional displays and scenes of such thunderous impact as a son showing a blind father how to commit suicide by jumping off a nonexistent cliff, or a deranged father trying to persuade his dead daughter to return to life?

To be intensely virtuosic in its dramatic displays, notably in the play's first three acts, necessarily involves a special dramatic structure. Virtually all commentators have noted that *Lear*'s greatness is surely different, and the nature of that differentness has been explained in a wide range of ways.[4] Careful, detailed analysis of *Lear*'s dramatic structure will indicate, unsurprisingly, that although we may not have always or accurately understood him, Shakespeare knew exactly what he wanted to do. Plainly, so sweeping and pervasive a dedication to dramatic effect cannot be accidental. H. Granville Barker *almost* came to the exact conclusion that I will here assert, only to end on exactly the opposite side of the fence:"*It is possible that this most practical and loyal of dramatists did for once . . . break his promise and betray his trust by presenting to his fellows a play,* the capital parts of which they simply could not act."[5] It seems to me not only possible, but demonstrably correct that Shakespeare *did* intend to give his actor comrades a play—but a play that was specifically and consciously meant for them to, as the phrase goes, cut a rug. Insert a period instead of a comma, at the end of the italicized portion of Granville Barker's remarks, and you have precisely the argument I will now set out: *Lear*—at least in its first three acts—was from the start designed to indulge and please the actors in Shakespeare's company.

It is not accidental that, though the cast list is relatively small, twelve of *Lear*'s two dozen significant characters have *each* been awarded no less than 14 percent of the play's on-stage time (significant on-stage time, not including mere on-stage-presence). Ophelia, a famously important character in *Hamlet,* has only 17 percent. Further, no single character in *Lear,* Lear included, has anything like the dominant 66 percent of stage time given to Hamlet, the 64 percent given to Iago in *Othello,* or the 59 percent given to both Othello and Macbeth. Here is a roughly calculated list of on-stage time for *Lear*'s twelve most prominent characters:

Lear	48%
Kent	39.4%
Gloucester	36.5%
Edgar	33%
Edmund	24%

Fool	21%
Goneril	20.5%
Regan	20.5%
Albany	17%
Cornwall	17%
Oswald	14%
Cordelia	11%

Each of these parts is what actors call a "fat" role, any one of which could be honorably undertaken by a theatrical "star." If, once again, this is not accidental, why has Shakespeare been thus unprecedentedly generous to his actors?

Consider, in the order of their first appearance on stage, the range of emotions displayed by eleven of the above-listed twelve prominent characters (Cornwall's first-act appearance is almost totally nonverbal), in the sequence of their appearances in the first act.

Kent: (1) gentlemanly, considerate, (2) forthright, intrepid, determined, loyal, (3) peasant-like in dress and dogged, blunt speech, (3) clever with peasant-appropriate words, (4) ferociously, violently upper-class-conscious

Gloucester: (1) courtly, bawdy, paternal, (2) dutiful, (3) aggravated, distressed, conspiratorial, philosophically self-important

Edmund: (1) humble, filial, (2) soaringly self-advancing, provocative, hypocritically unctuous, contemptuous, brazenly lying

Lear: (1) majestic, credulous, tempestuously hasty, punitive, violent, heavily sarcastic, cruel, (2) affable, imperious, shocked, violent, grateful, detached, brisk, unbelieving,

bewildered, ironic, angry, confused, threatening, indignant,
(3) business-like, repentant, shaky

Goneril: (1) flagrantly flattering, righteously scornful, disloyal,
conspiratorial, pompous, (2) imperious, arrogant,
commanding, lying, (3) aggressive, condescending, cruel,
relentless, haughty

Cordelia: (1) moralistic, rigidly, inflexibly filial, sorrowful,
stern, pedagogically inclined

Regan: (1) flagrantly flattering, righteously scornful, disloyal,
conspiratorial, pompous

Edgar: (1) courtly, fraternal, credulous, confused

Oswald: (1) oily, subservient, indignant, proud

Fool: (1) sadly mocking, witty, quick, prophetic, truthful,
musical (he sings), class-conscious, observant, dance-like
(he mimes), pathetic, meditative

Albany: (1) courtly, shocked, politely firm, quietly truthful,
philosophical

Shakespeare is notorious, to be sure, for presenting us with a busy
stage. His characters are invariably in constant motion. Only the
fast and furious mood-shifting shared, appropriately, by Lear and
Kent is distinctly unusual, but the aggregate degree of often very
abrupt changes in mood is noteworthy.

The tone of these characters, further, is as quick-triggered and
often as extravagant as their actions. It is Lear who first signals,
though he does not fully initiate, the play's tonal extravagance:

> Tell me, my daughters
> (Since now we will divest us both of rule,
> Interest of territory, cares of state),
> Which of you shall we say doth love us most,

That we our largest bounty may extend
Where nature doth with merit challenge.

(1.1.49–54)

Lear has been, to this point, "every inch a king" (as he says most pathetically, later in the play). His plan to give up power and divide his kingdom among his children seems businesslike and feasible—until this curiously bland idiocy. Shakespeare blows no trumpets, offers us no high-dramatic signals, but if there were time to stop and consider, when watching (or even when reading), it would surely seem extraordinary to have an apparently sober ruler declare that division of the realm will take place according to "which of you ... doth love us most." Love him most? The play has deftly slid away from sanity and into a never-never land of utter foolishness. And Goneril, oldest child and therefore the first to speak, winds up the rhetorical engines:

> Sir,
> I love you more than words can wield the matter,
> Dearer than eyesight, space, and liberty,
> Beyond what can be valued, rich or rare,
> No less than life, with grace, health, beauty, honor.
> As much as child e'er loved, or father found.
> A love that makes breath poor, and speech unable –
> Beyond all manner of so much I love you.

(1.1.55–62)

Even without the annotated explanations to be found in the text that follows, the profound emptiness of these vows is obvious. "I love you a whole lot," Goneril says, "a whole whole lot lot, a whole whole whole lot lot lot." The burden on the actress, here (the part having been played by a prepubescent boy, in Shakespeare's time), is to make the surface of this plausible, while simultaneously registering its inner flatulence.

And Lear does not bat an eyelash, swallowing this farrago of platitudes as if it meant something. Indeed, he promptly acts on it, and gives Goneril the rewards she wanted. Then, as if he is being completely businesslike and sober (though he is in fact already a candidate for an Alzheimer physician), he turns to Regan, asking: "What says our second daughter, / Our dearest Regan, wife to Cornwall? Speak." And she in essence repeats Goneril's high-order near-gibberish:

> I am made of that self mettle as my sister,
> And prize me at her worth. In my true heart
> I find she names my very deed of love,
> Only she comes too short. That I profess
> Myself an enemy to all other joys
> Which the most precious square of sense possesses,
> And find I am alone felicitate
> In your dear Highness' love.

> (1.1.71–78)

What can one say? Lear's reaction remains the same, and Regan too gets her share.

We have been prepared by Cordelia's brief asides, and we know she is exceedingly unlike her sisters. But Shakespeare spices matters by making Cordelia, and not the older daughters, the King's clear favorite:

> Now our joy,
> Although our last and least, to whose young love

The vines of France and milk of Burgundy
Strive to be of interest. What can you say to draw
A third more opulent than your sisters? Speak.

(1.1.84–88)

The "opulence" lathered on him by Goneril and Regan is plainly what he wants, but he anticipates still greater pleasure, hearing it from the child he favors. There follows the first part of their elaborate exchange:

Cordelia Nothing, my lord.
Lear   Nothing?
Cordelia Nothing.
Lear   Nothing will come of nothing, speak again.
Cordelia Unhappy that I am, I cannot heave
  My heart into my mouth. I love your Majesty
  According to my bond, no more nor less.
Lear   How now, Cordelia? Mend your speech a little,
  Lest you may mar your fortunes.

(1.1.89–97)

If Lear has been lost in a fantasy world, and Goneril and Regan have been swishing through a fog of pure verbality, Cordelia swings starkly to the other extreme. Lear's subsequent unbalanced rage, no matter how predictable, is grandly dramatic—but what I want to emphasize is, quite simply, the poundingly dramatic absoluteness of both words and actions, in this whole flattery-milking affair. It is without question great theater. It stretches actors to their utmost. It thrills, moves, and ultimately enthralls viewers (and readers). "Virtuosic" is thus, here, another way of saying immense, extravagant, boldly impressive, intensely passionate.

But it may seem clearer, by now, that the difference between *Lear* and most of Shakespeare's other great plays is primarily founded on dramatic extravagance, beautifully handled, splendidly phrased, but not entirely the same kind of drama we find in *Hamlet, Othello,* or *Macbeth.* Until we reach act 4, and Shakespeare more or less "reverts" to his justly celebrated profound insights into human nature, *Lear*'s characters are of high interest *not* because of what they *are* but because of what they *do.* This not a value judgment. Grand opera, similarly extravagant, is no less artistically potent than the wry plays of Anton Chekhov or the grinding, partly bewildering, but always enlightening plays of Samuel Beckett. Grand opera is simply by its very nature different from merely verbal drama.

Lear is every bit as experimental, and as breath-taking, as *Macbeth.* There is an immense amount of witty speech, and not a little burlesque, in *Hamlet.* There is a streak of mordant wit in *Othello,* but nothing particularly burlesque. There is almost no witty speech in *Macbeth,* and no burlesque: as I have noted, in my edition of that play, the porter at the gate scene is deadly serious. None of the mentioned mature plays has the fantastical material of *The Tempest.* None has the satirical bite, the social sweep, of *Twelfth Night.* We do not have to choose among them, or appreciate one less because we appreciate any or all of the others.

But Shakespeare's purpose, in the experiment that is the first three acts of *Lear,* may now have become plainer. I have said that the first three acts of the play are actor-oriented: for most of the play, it is a grandness of acting that is plainly the playwright's largest concern. Did Shakespeare conceive this emphasis on his own, or collaboratively with the other, more actively on-stage members of his company? There is no direct evidence, nor does it, I think, make a great deal of difference. As in most things, there is almost certain to be a complex mixture of motivations. Actors may have complained, or petitioned. This was a collectively sustained stage, in ways that it is sometimes hard for us to understand. Not only was there no director, but neither was there a stage manager, or a set designer, or a costume designer, or a lighting expert, or a soundman. From what we know of rehearsals, they were rarely if ever full run-throughs. Actors rehearsed *their* scenes, not whole plays. We do not know how closely the acting "scripts" that we have resemble either the original manuscripts, or whether or not there ever were such things as preliminary, unacted versions. We do not know, as I note in the "Textual Note," below, at what stage in a particular play's history the version (or versions) we have were drafted, or in whose hand. Or by whose direction. It seems clear that the 1623 Folio had no "editor," in our sense of the word. And there are many equally uncertain matters we need to confront as directly as we can. But we neither have, nor can we reasonably expect ever to have, all the answers to all our pressing questions.

And the only legitimate answer to why Shakespeare changed the dramatic nature of the play, after act 3, is "yes." That is, Shakespeare did it: that is all we know and, of necessity, all we need to know.

A word is in order, as to Shakespeare's sources for *Lear.* Like the Greek dramatists almost two thousand years earlier, Shakespeare was a notorious plot-borrower. Many of the ways in which his narratives varied from their sources are, from play to play, of considerable interest; nothing Shakespeare does is of no interest. But what is particularly illuminating, in the case of *Lear,* is the nature and quality of its sources, which start as ancient folktale and develop into a kind of popular "history." That is, the intrinsic simpleness of *Lear*'s sources, which display a traditional absence of psychological complexities, may have given Shakespeare the freedom required, in order to focus on *what* happened rather than *how* or *why*. *Lear* has always reminded commentators of the "fairy tale" it once was. The pain and suffering in fairy tales is undeniable. But it is not the pain and suffering of Fyodor Dostoyevsky, or Franz Kafka—or that of *Hamlet*. Again, that is not a value judgment but a fact.

Notes

1. A. C. Bradley, *Shakespearean Tragedy: Lectures on Hamlet, Othello, King Lear, Macbeth* (London: Macmillan, 1961), 198–99.
2. Jan Kott, *Shakespeare Our Contemporary* (New York: Norton, 1974), 127.
3. Margaret Webster, *Shakespeare Without Tears* (New York: Whittelsey House, 1942), 221, 223, 224.
4. Commentators have, indeed, fairly stood on their heads, trying to justify *Lear*'s differentness: "The tragedy is most poignant in that it is purposeless, unreasonable. . . . *King Lear* is supreme in that, in [its] main theme, it faces the very absence of tragic purpose." G. Wilson Knight, *The Wheel of Fire: Interpretations of Shakespearean Tragedy* (New York: Meridian Books, 1957), 174–175.
5. H. Granville Barker, "King Lear," quoted in Anne Bradby, ed., *Shakespeare Criticism, 1919–35* (London: Oxford University Press, 1936), 112.

TEXTUAL NOTE

*K*ing *Lear* has two differing printed texts, the 1608 Quarto and the 1623 Folio. (I need not here discuss the so-called Second Quarto, falsely dated 1608 but in fact printed in 1619 and pretty much a copy of the 1608 text.) We do not know and are likely never to know how distant each of the two texts is from Shakespeare's original, though that is hardly a unique bepuzzlement. On the evidence of the two texts themselves, there is no reason to believe that there are or ever were two distinct versions of the play. The Quarto is obviously more carelessly printed: there are 167 differences among its twelve surviving copies. This is not gross carelessness, by Elizabethan standards of printing, but it is definitely on the high side. The Folio is much more carefully printed, and in addition to correcting many errors (and adding not a few of its own), it does a good deal of editing, most of it clearly both consistent and responsible. It adds a total of 115 lines to the Quarto text, and deletes a total of 265 lines.

On the evidence of the two texts, the most sensible and conservative editorial position seems to be that, when possible, the Folio text should be reproduced. It may or may be not based on an authoritative manuscript (there are no manuscripts for any of

Shakespeare's surviving plays, nor do we know without question on what kind of texts any of his plays has been based). Most commentators, and an even higher percentage of those who have actually collated the two texts, would probably agree that, though the Quarto is imperfect, and the Folio is markedly superior, the Folio is not a perfect "copy text" (that is, the text on which an edition is based). Accordingly, the only editorial perspective other than that just stated would be the highly speculative and I think incorrect conclusion that these two printed texts are distinct versions.

Some few of the passages deleted in the Folio, having become embedded in readers' minds, and in critical commentary, are here restored, either in whole or in part. Act 4, scene 3, is deleted in the Folio, a readily understandable omission for what is plainly a performance-oriented text. This edition, however, being a reading-oriented text, act 4, scene 3—characterologically and narratively enrichening—is here restored in its entirety. (The question of performance versus reading is charmingly and passionately discussed in Charles Lamb's famous essay "On the Tragedies of Shakespeare, Considered with Reference to Their Fitness for Stage-Representation.") All such restorations are identified in text footnotes.

As I have throughout the Annotated Shakespeare series, I here avoid emendations. An editor, in my judgment, should resort to such extreme solutions only in absolute desperation and never because he or she believes this or that word or phrase sounds better than what either of the two printed texts gives us. No matter how clever we are, we are not Shakespeare. The Folio editors were not Shakespeare either, but they were a great deal closer to him than we are, in both time and acquaintance.

SOME ESSENTIALS OF THE
SHAKESPEAREAN STAGE

The Stage

- There was no *scenery* (backdrops, flats, and so on).

- Compared to today's elaborate, high-tech productions, the Elizabethan stage had few *on-stage* props. These were mostly handheld: a sword or dagger, a torch or candle, a cup or flask. Larger props, such as furniture, were used sparingly.

- Costumes (some of which were upper-class castoffs, belonging to the individual actors) were elaborate. As in most premodern and very hierarchical societies, clothing was the distinctive mark of who and what a person was.

- What the actors *spoke,* accordingly, contained both the dramatic and narrative material we have come to expect in a theater (or movie house) and (1) the setting, including details of the time of day, the weather, and so on, and (2) the occasion. The *dramaturgy* is thus very different from that of our own time, requiring much more attention to verbal and gestural matters. Strict realism was neither intended nor, under the circumstances, possible.

- There was *no curtain*. Actors entered and left via doors in the back of the stage, behind which was the "tiring-room," where actors put on or changed their costumes.

- In *public theaters* (which were open-air structures), there was no *lighting;* performances could take place only in daylight hours.

- For *private* theaters, located in large halls of aristocratic houses, candlelight illumination was possible.

The Actors

- Actors worked in *professional,* for-profit companies, sometimes organized and owned by other actors, and sometimes by entrepreneurs who could afford to erect or rent the company's building. Public theaters could hold, on average, two thousand playgoers, most of whom viewed and listened while standing. Significant profits could be and were made. Private theaters were smaller, more exclusive.

- There was *no director.* A book-holder/prompter/props manager, standing in the tiring-room behind the backstage doors, worked from a text marked with entrances and exits and notations of any special effects required for that particular script. A few such books have survived. Actors had texts only of their own parts, speeches being cued to a few prior words. There were few and often no rehearsals, in our modern use of the term, though there was often some coaching of individuals. Since Shakespeare's England was largely an oral culture, actors learned their parts rapidly and retained them for years. This was *repertory* theater, repeating popular plays and introducing some new ones each season.

- *Women* were not permitted on the professional stage. Most female roles were acted by *boys;* elderly women were played by grown men.

The Audience

- London's professional theater operated in what might be called a "red-light" district, featuring brothels, restaurants, and the kind of *open-air entertainment* then most popular, like bear-baiting (in which a bear, tied to a stake, was set on by dogs).

- A theater audience, like most of the population of Shakespeare's England, was largely made up of *illiterates.* Being able to read and write, however, had nothing to do with intelligence or concern with language, narrative, and characterization. People attracted to the theater tended to be both extremely verbal and extremely volatile. Actors were sometimes attacked, when the audience was dissatisfied; quarrels and fights were relatively common. Women were regularly in attendance, though no reliable statistics exist.

- Drama did not have the cultural esteem it has in our time, and plays were not regularly printed. Shakespeare's often appeared in book form, but not with any supervision or other involvement on his part. He wrote a good deal of nondramatic poetry as well, yet so far as we know he did not authorize or supervise *any* work of his that appeared in print during his lifetime.

- Playgoers, who had paid good money to see and hear, plainly gave dramatic performances careful, detailed attention. For some closer examination of such matters, see Burton Raffel, "Who Heard the Rhymes and How: Shakespeare's Dramaturgical Signals," *Oral Tradition* 11 (October 1996): 190–221, and Raffel, "Metrical Dramaturgy in Shakespeare's Earlier Plays," *CEA Critic* 57 (Spring–Summer 1995): 51–65.

King Lear

CHARACTERS (DRAMATIS PERSONAE)

Lear (King of Britain)

Goneril, Regan,[1] *Cordelia* (Lear's daughters)

Duke[2] *of Albany* (Goneril's husband)

Duke of Cornwall (Regan's husband)

Earl[3] *of Kent*

Earl of Gloucester[4]

Edgar (Gloucester's older son)

Edmund (Gloucester's younger son, illegitimate)

King of France

Duke of Burgundy

Fool

Oswald (Goneril's steward)

Curran (Gloucester's servant)

Old Man, Doctor, Captain, Herald, Knights, Messengers, Servants, Soldiers

1 RAYgin
2 duke = nobleman of royal blood, subordinate only to a king
3 earl = nobleman of lesser rank than a duke (often not a hereditary rank)
4 GLAHster

Act I

SCENE I

King Lear's palace

ENTER KENT, GLOUCESTER, AND EDMUND

Kent   I thought the King had more affected[1] the Duke of
Albany than Cornwall.

Gloucester It did always seem so to us.[2] But now, in the division
of the kingdom, it appears not[3] which of the dukes he values[4]
most, for qualities[5] are so weighed[6] that curiosity[7] in neither[8]   5
can make choice[9] of either's moiety.[10]

Kent   Is not this your son, my lord?

---

1 more affected = better liked
2 me (the royal "we," employed by many highborn figures in this play)★
3 appears not = is not clear/visible
4 esteems★
5 capacities, characteristics★
6 balanced, calculated
7 ingenuity, careful attention
8 neither one of the two dukes
9 make choice = choose
10 either's moiety = the other duke's share/portion

Gloucester His breeding,[11] sir, hath been at my charge.[12] I have
so often blushed to acknowledge him, that now I am brazed
to[13] it.

Kent   I cannot conceive[14] you.

Gloucester Sir, this young fellow's mother could,[15] whereupon
she grew round-wombed, and had (indeed) sir a son for her
cradle, ere[16] she had a husband for her bed. Do you smell a
fault?[17]

Kent   I cannot wish the fault undone, the issue[18] of it being
so proper.[19]

Gloucester But I have a son, sir, by order of law,[20] some year[21]
elder than this, who yet is no dearer[22] in my account,[23]
though this knave[24] came something saucily[25] into the world
before he was sent for. Yet was his mother fair,[26] there was
good sport[27] at his making, and the whoreson[28] must be

---

11 education, bringing up★
12 responsibility, expense
13 brazed to = hardened to, shameless about
14 understand, comprehend
15 become pregnant ("conceive")
16 before
17 smell a fault = perceive/suspect a moral wrong★
18 (1) offspring, (2) outcome★
19 more (1) worthy/admirable, (2) handsome
20 by order of law = under the sacrament/arrangement of marriage (i.e.,
   Edgar is legitimate)
21 some year = about/roughly a year
22 worthier, esteemed, valued, beloved★
23 (1) estimation, opinion, (2) reckoning, calculations
24 rascal★ (Edmund)
25 something saucily = rather/to some extent★ impertinently/cheekily/
   rudely★
26 good-looking, beautiful★
27 entertainment, recreation, amorous dalliance
28 bastard (here, jocular)★

acknowledged.[29] Do you know this noble gentleman, Edmund?

Edmund   No, my lord.   25

Gloucester   My Lord of Kent. Remember him hereafter as my honorable friend.

Edmund   My services[30] to your lordship.

Kent   I must love[31] you, and sue[32] to know you better.

Edmund   Sir, I shall study deserving.[33]   30

Gloucester   He hath been out[34] nine years, and away he shall[35] again.

SENNET[36]

The King is coming.

ENTER KING LEAR, CORNWALL, ALBANY, GONERIL, REGAN, CORDELIA, AND ATTENDANTS

Lear   Attend[37] the lords of France and Burgundy, Gloucester.   35

Gloucester   I shall, my liege.[38]

EXEUNT GLOUCESTER AND EDMUND

29 recognized, confessed (unacknowledged children were not legally regarded as a father's offspring)
30 respects, compliments
31 regard, like
32 (1) proceed, (2) seek
33 study deserving = apply myself★ to earning/being entitled/worthy★
34 out of the country, away
35 must
36 fanfare
37 wait upon
38 address by a subordinate to his superior (originally a feudal acknowledgment)

Lear Meantime we shall express[39] our darker purpose.[40]
　　　Give me the map there.[41] Know,[42] that we have divided
　　　In three our kingdom. And 'tis our fast[43] intent
40　　To shake[44] all cares and business[45] from our age,[46]
　　　Conferring them on younger strengths, while we
　　　Unburthened crawl toward death. Our son[47] of Cornwall,
　　　And you, our no less loving son of Albany,
　　　We have this hour[48] a constant will[49] to publish[50]
45　　Our daughters' several dowers,[51] that[52] future strife
　　　May be prevented now. The princes,[53] France and Burgundy,
　　　Great rivals in[54] our youngest daughter's love,
　　　Long in our court[55] have made their amorous sojourn,[56]
　　　And here are to be answered.[57] Tell me, my daughters

39 set forth, convey, reveal
40 darker purpose = more unknowable/secret/hidden determination/
   intention★
41 map there: (?) that map there, *or* (?) you over there
42 be made aware, understand, learn
43 firm, fixed
44 shake off, dislodge, get rid of
45 cares and business = troubles/anxieties/concerns★ and labor/activities/
   exertions★
46 old age
47 relationships created by marriage were spoken of in the same terms as birth
   relationships
48 this hour = now
49 constant will = resolute/steadfast desire/wish
50 make public/generally known
51 several dowers = distinct/different★ dowries (money/property conveyed in
   marriage by the wife/her family to the husband)★
52 so that
53 persons of royal standing
54 as to, in the matter of ("for")
55 i.e., those who surround a monarch ("courtiers")
56 temporary stay
57 responded to ("given an answer")★

(Since now we will divest us both[58] of rule,   50
Interest of[59] territory, cares of state),
Which of you shall we say doth love us most,
That[60] we our largest bounty may extend[61]
Where nature doth with merit challenge.[62] Goneril,
Our eldest-born, speak first.   55

Goneril Sir,
I love you more than words can wield[63] the matter,[64]
Dearer than eyesight, space,[65] and liberty,[66]
Beyond[67] what can be valued, rich[68] or rare,
No less than life, with grace,[69] health, beauty, honor.[70]   60
As much as child e'er loved, or father found.[71]
A love that makes breath poor,[72] and speech unable[73] –
Beyond all manner of so much[74] I love you.

---

58 i.e., loosely plural, not limited to precisely two of something
59 interest of = legal title in
60 so that
61 bounty may extend = generosity can direct to
62 nature doth with merit challenge = birth and worthiness/deserving dispute
   with one another
63 manage, deal with, utter
64 thoughts, substance ("subject matter")★
65 living space/room/scope
66 the right to do as one thinks best
67 more than
68 whether rich
69 favor, fortune★
70 no LESS than LIFE with GRACE health BEAUty ONor
71 encountered, met with (as MUCH as CHILD e'er LOVED or FAther
   FOUND)
72 breath poor = (?) (1) the capacity for breathing inadequate, *or* (2) words/
   language inadequate (the 2nd meaning would clearly be the proper choice,
   except that Shakespeare immediately and additively refers to "speech")
73 incompetent, ineffectual
74 all manner of so much = all such comparisons

Cordelia (*aside*) What shall[75] Cordelia speak? Love, and be silent.

65 *Lear*   (*referring to map*) Of all these bounds,[76] even[77] from this
         line, to this,
         With shadowy[78] forests and with champains riched[79]
         With plenteous[80] rivers, and wide-skirted meads,[81]
         We make thee lady.[82] To thine and Albany's issue
         Be this perpetual.[83] What says our second daughter,
70   Our dearest Regan, wife to Cornwall? Speak.

    Regan   I am made of that self mettle[84] as my sister,[85]
         And prize me[86] at her worth.[87] In my true[88] heart
         I find she names my very deed[89] of love,
         Only she comes too short.[90] That[91] I profess[92]
75   Myself an enemy to all other joys
         Which the most precious square[93] of sense possesses,
         And find I am alone felicitate[94]

75 must
76 boundary lines
77 exactly, equally
78 shady
79 champains riched = level, open country/fields enriched
80 abundant, plentiful
81 wide-skirted meads = wide-edged/bordered meadows
82 owner (female counterpart of "lord")
83 yours forever
84 self mettle = same disposition/temperament/spirit
85 i am MADE of THAT self MEtle AS my SISter
86 prize me = account/value/esteem★ myself
87 (1) price, value, (2) excellence★
88 (1) trusty, loyal, faithful, firm, (2) real, certain★
89 action, performance
90 comes too short = does not deal with it adequately★
91 because
92 declare, vow, affirm
93 standard, rule, measure (right-angle carpenter's tool)
94 alone felicitate = only made happy

In your dear Highness' love.

Cordelia   (*aside*) Then poor Cordelia!
   And yet not so, since I am sure my love's
   More ponderous[95] than my tongue.   80

Lear   To thee and thine hereditary ever
   Remain this ample third of our fair kingdom,
   No less in space, validity, and pleasure
   Than that conferred on Goneril. Now our joy,
   Although our last and least,[96] to whose young love   85
   The vines of France and milk[97] of Burgundy
   Strive to be of interest.[98] What can you say to draw
   A third more opulent[99] than your sisters? Speak.

Cordelia Nothing, my lord.

Lear   Nothing?   90

Cordelia Nothing.

Lear   Nothing will come of nothing, speak again.

Cordelia Unhappy that I am, I cannot heave[100]
   My heart into my mouth. I love your Majesty
   According to my bond,[101] no more nor less.   95

Lear   How now, Cordelia? Mend[102] your speech a little,
   Lest you may mar your fortunes.[103]

Cordelia   Good my lord,

---

95 weighty, massive
96 (1) shortest, smallest, (2) youngest
97 abundance, riches (as in the biblical "milk and honey")
98 of interest = legally connected ("married")
99 splendid, rich (i.e., not in size but in value)
100 lift up, raise, move
101 duty, obligation
102 improve, reform, correct
103 (1) prosperity, (2) chances, luck★

You have begot[104] me, bred me, loved me. I
Return[105] those duties back as are right fit,[106]
100   Obey you, love you, and most[107] honor you.
Why have my sisters husbands, if they say
They love you all?[108] Haply,[109] when I shall wed,
That lord[110] whose hand must take my plight[111] shall carry
Half my love with him, half my care and duty.[112]
105   Sure, I shall never marry like my sisters,
To love my father all.

Lear   But goes thy heart with this?

Cordelia   Ay, good my lord.

Lear   So young, and so untender?[113]

Cordelia   So young, my lord, and true.

110 *Lear*   Let it be so, thy truth then be thy dower.
For by the sacred radiance of the sun,
The mysteries of Hecate[114] and the night,
By all the operation of the orbs[115]
From whom we do exist and cease to be,
115   Here I disclaim[116] all my paternal care,

---

104 called into being, procreated ("fathered")
105 reverse, reciprocate ("turn back to you")
106 right fit = completely/precisely★ proper/appropriate/suitable★
107 most of all
108 entirely, exclusively
109 perhaps
110 husband ("lord" of a household)
111 plight = plighting = marriage vows
112 (1) respect, deference, (2) obligation, responsibility★
113 unkind, unsoft, unloving, tough ("stiff-necked")
114 moon goddess, associated with witchcraft: Lear proclaims himself pagan rather than Christian (HEHkate)
115 celestial spheres within which all heavenly bodies moved, in Ptolemaic astronomy
116 formally/legally renounce/relinquish/repudiate★

Propinquity[117] and property of blood,[118]

And as a stranger to my heart and me

Hold thee from this[119] for ever. The barbarous Scythian,

Or he that makes his generation messes[120]

To gorge[121] his appetite, shall to my bosom   120

Be as well neighbored,[122] pitied, and relieved,[123]

As thou my sometime[124] daughter.

Kent   Good my liege –

Lear Peace,[125] Kent!

Come not between the dragon and his wrath.

I loved her most, and thought to set my rest[126]   125

On her kind nursery.[127] (*to Cordelia*) Hence, and avoid[128] my

sight!

So be my grave my peace, as here[129] I give[130]

Her father's heart from[131] her! Call[132] France: who stirs?[133]

Call Burgundy. Cornwall and Albany,

---

117 kinship ("closeness")

118 property of blood = rights/qualities of descent/blood relationship

119 now ("this time")

120 his generation messes = children into food/meals

121 feed, glut

122 close, friendly

123 helped, assisted

124 once, former

125 be silent★

126 (1) venture the rest/remainder of my life, (2) establish my residence/repose

127 care (as of a child)

128 stay out of, leave

129 so be my grave my peace, as here = just as I wish my grave to be the place where I am at peace, so too I here/hereby

130 (1) devise, award (as in a last will and testament), (2) make known, publish

131 away from

132 summon, command the attendance of

133 who stirs = (?) (1) why is no one hurrying to obey me? *or* (2) obey me!

130 With[134] my two daughters' dowers digest[135] the third.
Let pride, which she calls plainness,[136] marry her.[137]
I do invest you jointly with[138] my power,
Pre-eminence,[139] and all the large effects[140]
That troop with[141] majesty. Ourself, by monthly course,[142]
135 With reservation[143] of an hundred knights,
By you[144] to be sustained, shall our abode
Make with you by due turns, only we shall retain
The name, and all th' addition to[145] a king.
The sway,[146] revenue,[147] execution[148] of the rest,
140 Belovèd sons be yours, which to confirm,
This coronet part[149] betwixt you.

LEAR GIVES ALBANY AND CORNWALL HIS CROWN

Kent   Royal Lear,
Whom I have ever honored as my king,
Loved as my father, as my master followed,[150]

134 along with
135 divide, distribute
136 frankness, honesty, directness★
137 marry her = marry her off, take care of arranging her marriage
138 invest . . . with = settle . . . upon
139 high rank / distinction
140 consequences, manifestations★
141 troop with = are associated with
142 movement, circulation
143 holding back / retention★
144 i.e., I ("ourself") am to be supported / provided for / maintained . . . by you
145 addition to = marks of honor belonging to
146 rule, sovereign power★
147 reVENue
148 performance, carrying into effect
149 small, less exalted crown (KORnet) share
150 served★

As my great patron thought on[151] in my prayers —
Lear The bow is bent and drawn, make from[152] the shaft.[153]   145
Kent Let it fall rather, though the fork invade[154]

The region of my heart. Be Kent[155] unmannerly,
When Lear is mad. What wilt thou do, old man?
Think'st thou that duty shall have dread[156] to speak,
When power to flattery bows? To plainness honor's bound,   150
When majesty stoops[157] to folly. Reserve thy state,[158]
And in thy best consideration check[159]
This hideous rashness. Answer my life[160] my judgment.[161]
Thy youngest daughter does not love thee least,
Nor are those empty-hearted whose low sounds   155
Reverb[162] no hollowness.[163]

Lear   Kent, on thy life, no more.
Kent My life I never held but as a pawn[164]

To wage against thy enemies, nor fear to lose it,
Thy safety being the motive.

Lear   Out of my sight!
Kent See better, Lear, and let me still remain   160

151 patron thought on = lord/master/superior considered, remembered
152 make from = go/get away from
153 arrow
154 fork invade = the fork of the arrowhead penetrate to
155 be Kent = let Kent be
156 shall have dread = must be afraid
157 descends, falls
158 status, position
159 stop, retard★
160 answer my life = let my life suffer the consequences
161 (1) opinion, criticism, (2) discernment, reasoning★
162 reverberate/echo with
163 internal emptiness, insincerity★
164 i.e., as in chess, where pawns form the major defense of the king

The true blank[165] of thine eye.

Lear Now, by Apollo –

Kent   Now, by Apollo, King,

Thou swear'st[166] thy gods in vain.

Lear   O vassal![167] Miscreant![168]

LEAR PUTS HIS HAND ON HIS SWORD

Albany, Cornwall (*to Lear*) Dear sir, forbear.[169]

165 *Kent*   Kill thy physician, and the fee bestow

Upon[170] the foul[171] disease. Revoke thy gift,

Or whilst I can vent clamor[172] from my throat,

I'll tell thee thou dost evil.

Lear   Hear me, recreant![173]

On thine allegiance,[174] hear me!

170 Since thou hast sought to make us break our vows,

Which we durst[175] never yet, and with strainèd[176] pride

To come between our sentences[177] and our power,

---

165 center (white spot) of a target
166 swear by, appeal to
167 subordinate, servant (i.e., though a duke, Kent is the feudal inferior of the King)
168 wretch, rascal
169 (1) be patient ("control yourself"), (2) desist from violence ("avoid/shun this")★
170 bestow upon = apply/give to
171 offensive, filthy, gross★
172 vent clamor = utter/express opposition/complaint ("outcry")
173 oath-breaker, deserter
174 on thine allegiance = in the name of your sworn oath of obedience/faithfulness to me
175 have been so bold
176 with strainèd = you seek, with overzealous
177 decisions, judgments, decrees

Which nor our nature[178] nor our place[179] can bear,
Our potency made good,[180] take thy reward.
Five days we do allot thee, for provision[181]   175
To shield thee from diseases of the world,[182]
And on the sixth to[183] turn thy hated back
Upon our kingdom. If on the tenth day following,
Thy banished trunk[184] be found in our dominions,
The moment is thy death. Away! By Jupiter,   180
This shall not be revoked.

Kent Fare thee well, King. Sith[185] thus thou wilt appear,
Freedom lives hence, and banishment is here.
(*to Cordelia*) The[186] gods to their dear shelter[187] take thee,
maid,
That justly think'st, and hast most rightly said.   185
(*to Regan and Goneril*) And your large[188] speeches may your
deeds approve,[189]
That good effects may spring from words of love.
Thus Kent, O princes, bids you all adieu,
He'll shape his old course[190] in a country new.

178 nor our nature = neither my character/disposition★
179 rank, dignity, station, position
180 potency made good = authority/power demonstrated/enforced
181 preparation, arrangements
182 diseases of the world = worldly discomforts/troubles
183 are to/must
184 body ("person")
185 since
186 may the
187 protection
188 lavish
189 make good, confirm, demonstrate★
190 path, direction, customary ways★

EXIT KENT

FLOURISH[191]

ENTER GLOUCESTER, WITH FRANCE, BURGUNDY,
AND ATTENDANTS

190 *Gloucester* Here's France and Burgundy, my noble lord.
    Lear   My lord of Burgundy,
    We first address toward[192] you, who with this king
    Hath rivaled for our daughter. What in the least[193]
    Will you require[194] in present dower with[195] her,
    Or[196] cease your quest of[197] love?
195 *Burgundy*   Most royal Majesty,
    I crave[198] no more than hath your Highness offered,
    Nor will you tender[199] less.
    Lear   Right[200] noble Burgundy,
    When she was dear to us, we did hold[201] her so,
    But now her price is fallen. Sir, there she stands.
200   If aught within that little-seeming[202] substance,
    Or all of it, with our displeasure pieced,[203]

191 fanfare
192 address toward = speak to
193 in the least = in the smallest amount
194 request, ask for, demand, desire
195 present dower with = ready, in hand ("immediate") dower along with
196 or otherwise
197 for
198 ask, wish for★
199 offer
200 most, altogether (i.e., polite form of address)
201 believe, consider, think
202 little-seeming = small-appearing/looking physical being
203 joined

And nothing more, may fitly like[204] your Grace,[205]
She's there,[206] and she is yours.

Burgundy   I know no answer.[207]

Lear   Will you, with those infirmities she owes,[208]
Unfriended, new adopted to[209] our hate,   205
Dowered with our curse, and strangered[210] with our oath,
Take her, or leave her?

Burgundy   Pardon me, royal sir.
Election makes not up[211] on such conditions.

Lear   Then leave her, sir, for by the power that made me,
I tell you all her wealth. (*to France*) For you, great King,   210
I would not[212] from your love[213] make such a stray
To[214] match you where I hate, therefore beseech[215] you
To avert[216] your liking a more worthier way
Than on a wretch whom Nature is ashamed
Almost t'acknowledge hers.

France   This is most strange,   215
That she that even but now was your best object,[217]

204 fitly like = appropriately please
205 courtesy title extended to dukes and duchesses (as "Majesty" is used for a
    sovereign)★
206 she's there = there she is
207 I know no answer = I do not know how to answer
208 infirmities she owes = weaknesses/ flaws she possesses ("owns")
209 unfriended, new adopted to = friendless, having recently/newly received
210 alienated, made a stranger to me★
211 election makes not up = a choice cannot be formed/produced/prepared/
    decided
212 would not = do not wish to
213 i.e., referring to the relationship between Lear and France
214 stray to = departure/wandering/straying as to
215 I beg
216 turn
217 best object = drew your most attention/admiration

The argument[218] of your praise, balm of your age,[219]
Most best, most dearest, should in this trice[220] of time
Commit a thing so monstrous, to dismantle[221]

220   So many folds[222] of favor. Sure[223] her offense
Must be of such unnatural degree,
That monsters it,[224] or your fore-vouched[225] affection
Fall into taint,[226] which to believe of her
Must be a faith[227] that reason without[228] miracle
Could never plant in me.

225 *Cordelia* (*to Lear*) I yet beseech your Majesty –
If for I want[229] that glib and oily art,
To speak and purpose not,[230] since what I well intend
I'll do't before I speak – that you make known
It is no vicious blot,[231] murder, or foulness,

230   No unchaste action or dishonored step[232]
That hath deprived me of your grace and favor,
But even for want of that for which I am richer,

---

218 subject matter
219 balm of your age = soothing/restorative element of your old age
220 instant
221 strip away
222 layers, aspects
223 surely
224 monsters it = (verb) makes it monstrous
225 or your fore-vouched = or makes your previously displayed/declared/
    asserted
226 (1) disgrace, dishonor, (2) decay
227 belief
228 reason without = logic/mind★ absent a
229 for I want = because I lack★
230 purpose not = do not intend to do
231 fault, failing
232 deed, action

A still-soliciting[233] eye, and such a tongue

As I am glad I have not, though not to have it

Hath lost[234] me in your liking.

Lear   Better thou   235

Hadst not been born than not t'have pleased me better.

France   Is it but this? A tardiness in[235] nature

Which often leaves the history[236] unspoke

That it intends to do? My Lord of Burgundy,

What say you[237] to the lady? Love's not love   240

When it is mingled with regards[238] that stand

Aloof from the entire[239] point. Will you have her?

She is herself a dowry.

Burgundy   Royal Lear,

Give but that portion[240] which yourself proposed,

And here I take Cordelia by the hand,   245

Duchess of Burgundy.

Lear   Nothing, I have sworn, I am firm.

Burgundy (*to Cordelia*)[241] I am sorry, then, you have so[242] lost a father

That you must lose a husband.

Cordelia   Peace be[243] with Burgundy.

233 still-soliciting = always seeking/urging/importuning
234 ruined, destroyed
235 of
236 story, tale
237 what say you = how do you respond
238 particulars, concerns, considerations
239 undivided ("pure, central")
240 (1) share, (2) dowry, settlement
241 note that, though Burgundy refuses to speak directly to France, he speaks
   very directly to Cordelia
242 to such an extent
243 peace be = may you be at peace/well

250   Since that respects[244] of fortune are his love,
         I shall[245] not be his wife.
       France Fairest Cordelia, that art most rich, being poor;
         Most choice, forsaken,[246] and most loved, despised.
         Thee and thy virtues here I seize upon,
255   Be it[247] lawful I take up what's cast away.
         Gods, gods! 'Tis strange that from[248] their cold'st neglect[249]
         My love should kindle to inflamed respect.[250]
         Thy dowerless daughter, King, thrown to my chance,
         Is queen of us, of ours, and our fair France.
260   Not all the dukes of waterish[251] Burgundy
         Can buy this unprized[252] precious maid of [253] me.
         Bid them farewell, Cordelia, though unkind.[254]
         Thou losest here a better where[255] to find.
       Lear   Thou hast her France, let her be thine, for we
265   Have no such daughter, nor shall ever see
         That face of hers again. (*to Cordelia*) Therefore be gone,
         Without our grace, our love, our benison.[256]
         Come, noble Burgundy.

244 matters
245 (1) must, (2) will (note that Cordelia's blunt tongue is not reserved solely
     for her father)
246 most choice, forsaken = most exquisite / excellent, when forsaken
247 be it = if / since it is
248 because of
249 slighting
250 regard, consideration, partiality, esteem
251 damp
252 unvalued
253 from
254 though unkind = though they are (1) ungenerous, harsh, (2) unnatural
255 (noun) place
256 blessing

FLOURISH

EXEUNT ALL BUT FRANCE, GONERIL, REGAN,
AND CORDELIA

France   Bid farewell to your sisters.

Cordelia   The jewels[257] of our father, with washèd eyes[258]   270
   Cordelia leaves you. I know you what you are,
   And like[259] a sister am most loath to call[260]
   Your faults as they are named. Use[261] well our father.
   To your professèd[262] bosoms I commit him.
   But yet, alas, stood I[263] within his grace,   275
   I would prefer[264] him to a better place.
   So farewell to you both.

Regan   Prescribe[265] not us our duties.

Goneril   Let your study
   Be to content your lord, who hath received you
   At fortune's alms.[266] You have obedience scanted,[267]   280
   And well are worth[268] the want that you have wanted.[269]

---

257 treasures, adornments ("favorites, darlings")
258 washed eyes = tear-filled eyes (the JEWels OF our FAther with WASHèd
      EYES)
259 as
260 proclaim, clearly speak
261 treat★
262 self-proclaiming/affirming
263 stood I = if I were still
264 put/place
265 ordain, lay down, dictate
266 charity, benefaction
267 withheld, diminished, neglected★
268 worthy, deserving
269 (1) lacked ("caused to be wanting"), (2) wished for (i.e., deliberately
      created)

Cordelia Time shall unfold what plaited[270] cunning hides.

Who[271] covers faults, at last[272] with shame derides.[273]

Well may you prosper!

France   Come, my fair Cordelia.

EXEUNT FRANCE AND CORDELIA

285 *Goneril* Sister, it is not a little[274] I have to say,

Of what most nearly appertains[275] to us both.

I think our father will hence tonight.[276]

Regan That's most certain, and with you. Next month with

us.

Goneril You see how full of changes his age is. The observation

290 we have made of it hath not[277] been little. He always loved

our sister most, and with what poor judgment he hath now

cast her off appears too grossly.[278]

Regan 'Tis the infirmity of his age. Yet he hath ever but

slenderly known himself.

295 *Goneril* The best and soundest[279] of his time[280] hath been but

rash. Then must we look[281] to receive from his age not alone

the imperfections of long-engraffed[282] condition, but

270 folded, doubled over, pleated

271 those who

272 at last = in the end

273 (?) with shame derides = (1) shame derides them (Quarto: shame them
derides), *or* (2) they progress from concealment to open derision

274 it is not a little = there is a lot

275 nearly appertains = intimately/particularly/closely is related/belongs

276 these three lines are set in verse, in Folio, but in prose, in Quarto

277 "not": from Quarto

278 appears too grossly = is visible/can be seen plainly/obviously

279 steadiest, healthiest ("least flawed")

280 years, life

281 expect

282 set, fixed

therewithal the unruly waywardness[283] that infirm and
choleric[284] years bring with them.

Regan   Such unconstant starts[285] are we like to have from him   300
as this of Kent's banishment.

Goneril   There is[286] further compliment of leave-taking
between France and him. Pray you,[287] let's hit[288] together. If
our father carry authority[289] with such dispositions as he
bears,[290] this last surrender[291] of his will but offend us.   305

Regan   We shall further think on't.

Goneril   We must do something, and i' the heat.[292]

EXEUNT

283 unruly waywardness = ungovernable/disorderly/undisciplined
    stubbornness/perversity/egocentricity
284 temperamental, hot-tempered, irascible, wrathful★
285 unconstant starts = fickle/changeable leaps/sudden movements★
286 i.e., Lear and France and their people are still being ceremonious with one
    another (says Goneril)
287 pray you = I ask you ("please")★
288 stay, agree
289 carry authority = manages/conducts/deals with power
290 such dispositions as he bears = the sort/kind of (1) arrangements/
    practices/measures, (2) ways of doing things
291 giving up property/power
292 i' the heat = intensely, soon

SCENE 2

Gloucester's castle

ENTER EDMUND, WITH A LETTER

Edmund Thou Nature[1] art my goddess, to thy law
My services are bound. Wherefore should I
Stand[2] in the plague[3] of custom, and permit
The curiosity[4] of nations to deprive me,
5   For that I am some twelve or fourteen moonshines
Lag of[5] a brother? Why bastard? Wherefore base?[6]
When my dimensions[7] are as well compact,[8]
My mind as generous,[9] and my shape as true,[10]
As honest madam's[11] issue? Why brand they us
10   With base? With baseness, bastardy? Base, base?
Who[12] in the lusty stealth[13] of nature take
More composition[14] and fierce quality[15]
Than doth, within[16] a dull, stale, tirèd bed,

1 physical Nature
2 stop, remain motionless, continue★
3 sickness, disease
4 scrupulousness, fastidiousness
5 moonshines lag of = months later than
6 (1) lowly, inferior, (2) illegitimate
7 bodily parts ("body")
8 put together (adjective)
9 (1) highborn, noble, (2) high-spirited
10 well-patterned, correct, right
11 honest madam's = respectable/honorable/decent★ married woman's
12 we who
13 lusty stealth = merry/handsome/delightful/vigorous sneakiness/
    underhandedness/thievery
14 take more composition = require more arranging/mutuality
15 fierce quality = high-spirited/passionate character/disposition/ability
16 in

Go to the creating[17] a whole tribe of fops,[18]

Got 'tween asleep and wake? Well then,   15

Legitimate Edgar, I must have your land.

Our father's love is[19] to the bastard Edmund

As to[20] th' legitimate. Fine word, legitimate.

Well, my legitimate, if this letter speed,[21]

And my invention thrive, Edmund the base   20

Shall to' th' legitimate.[22] I grow,[23] I prosper.

Now gods, stand up[24] for bastards![25]

ENTER GLOUCESTER

Gloucester Kent banished thus? And France in choler parted?

And the King gone tonight? Subscribed[26] his power,

Confined to exhibition?[27] All this done   25

Upon the gad?[28] Edmund, how now? What news?

Edmund   So please your lordship, none.

Gloucester Why so earnestly seek you to put up[29] that letter?

Edmund   I know no news, my lord.

17 creating of
18 fools, idiots, dullard★
19 goes / is given to
20 as to = just as to
21 succeed
22 to' th' legitimate = prevail over the legally entitled son (shall TO leGItiMIT:
   by prosodic convention, "th'" is reduced to metrical – though *not* lexical /
   syntactical – nonexistence by the apostrophe)
23 (1) flourish, (2) enlarge
24 defend, support
25 this speech is set as prose, in Quarto
26 signed away
27 confined to exhibition = limited to maintenance
28 upon the gad = on the move
29 away

30 *Gloucester* What paper[30] were you reading?

   Edmund   Nothing, my lord.

   Gloucester No? What needed then that terrible dispatch[31] of it
       into your pocket? The quality of nothing hath not such need
       to hide itself. Let's see.[32] Come, if it be nothing, I shall not
35   need spectacles.

   Edmund   I beseech you sir, pardon me.[33] It is a letter from my
       brother, that I have not all o'er-read,[34] and for so much as I
       have perused,[35] I find it not fit for your o'erlooking.

   Gloucester Give me the letter, sir.

40 *Edmund*   I shall offend, either to detain[36] or give it. The
       contents, as in part I understand them, are to blame.

   Gloucester Let's see, let's see.

   Edmund   I hope, for my brother's justification, he wrote this but
       as an essay or taste[37] of my virtue.

45 *Gloucester* (*reads*) "This policy, and reverence of[38] age, makes the
       world bitter to the best of our times,[39] keeps our fortunes
       from us till our oldness cannot relish them. I begin to find an
       idle and fond[40] bondage in the oppression of aged tyranny,
       who[41] sways not as[42] it hath power, but as it is suffered.[43]

30 document
31 hasty getting rid
32 let's see = let's have a look at it
33 pardon me = excuse me from showing it to you
34 o'er-read = read through
35 gone through, examined★
36 keep, withhold
37 essay or taste = test or trial/test
38 reverence of = respect★ for
39 best of our times = best years of our lives ("youth")
40 idle and fond = empty and foolish, sickly★
41 that
42 according to how
43 endured, submitted to

Come to me, that of this I may speak more. If our father   50
would sleep till I waked him,[44] you should enjoy half his
revenue[45] for ever, and live the beloved of your brother,
EDGAR."
Hum? Conspiracy? "Sleep till I wake him, you should enjoy
half his revenue." My son Edgar, had he a hand to write   55
this?[46] A heart and brain to breed[47] it in? When came this to
you? Who brought it?

Edmund   It was not brought me, my lord, there's the cunning[48]
of it. I found it thrown in at the casement of my closet.[49]

Gloucester   You know the character[50] to be your brother's?   60

Edmund   If the matter were good, my lord, I durst[51] swear it
were his. But in respect of[52] that, I would fain[53] think it were
not.

Gloucester   It is his.

Edmund   It is his hand, my lord. But I hope his heart is not in   65
the contents.

Gloucester   Hath he never heretofore sounded[54] you in this
business?

Edmund   Never, my lord. But I have heard him oft maintain it
to be fit that sons at perfect[55] age, and fathers declining, the   70

44 i.e., never, because he would be dead
45 income
46 i.e., was he actually able to write something like this?
47 give rise to, create
48 cleverness, skill
49 casement of my closet = window of my small private room ("study")
50 handwriting
51 dare, am so bold as to
52 in respect of = as regards/relates to
53 be glad to★
54 approached, questioned
55 fully grown, legally mature

father should be as ward[56] to the son, and the son manage his
revenue.

Gloucester O villain, villain. His very[57] opinion in the letter!
Abhorred[58] villain! Unnatural, detested, brutish[59] villain!
75   Worse than brutish! Go sirrah,[60] seek him. I'll apprehend[61]
him. Abominable villain! Where is he?

Edmund   I do not well know, my lord. If it shall please you to
suspend your indignation[62] against my brother, till you can
derive from him better testimony[63] of his intent, you shall
80   run a certain[64] course. Where,[65] if you violently proceed
against him, mistaking his purpose, it would make a great
gap[66] in your own honor, and shake in pieces the heart[67] of
his obedience. I dare pawn down[68] my life for him, that he
hath wrote this to feel[69] my affection to your honor, and to
85   no further pretense of danger.[70]

Gloucester Think you so?

Edmund   If your honor judge it meet,[71] I will place you where

56 a minor, requiring a guardian
57 exact
58 digusting, horrifying
59 savage ("animal-like")
60 mister (used by a superior speaking to an inferior)★
61 seize, arrest
62 wrath, anger
63 evidence, proof
64 fixed, precise, definite
65 whereas
66 (1) break, (2) wound, gash
67 center, seat, soul
68 pawn down = pledge
69 explore, examine
70 pretense of danger = dangerous purpose/intention
71 suitable, proper, appropriate★

you shall hear us confer of[72] this, and by an auricular[73]
assurance have your satisfaction, and that without any further
delay than this very evening.   90

Gloucester He cannot be such a monster. Edmund, seek him out.
Wind[74] me into him, I pray you. Frame[75] the business after[76]
your own wisdom. I would unstate myself,[77] to be in a due
resolution.[78]

Edmund   I will seek him, sir, presently,[79] convey[80] the business   95
as I shall find means, and acquaint you withal.

Gloucester These late[81] eclipses in the sun and moon portend[82]
no good to us. Though the wisdom of nature[83] can reason it
thus, and thus, yet nature finds itself scourged[84] by the
sequent[85] effects. Love cools, friendship falls off,[86] brothers   100
divide.[87] In cities, mutinies;[88] in countries, discord; in palaces,
treason; and the bond cracked 'twixt son and father. This
villain of mine comes under[89] the prediction: there's son

72 about
73 audible
74 twist, lead
75 prepare, shape
76 according to
77 I would unstate myself = I would be willing to give up my status/rank
78 to be in a due resolution = to have rightly/properly/truly solved/resolved
     this
79 at once★
80 guide, conduct, lead
81 recent★
82 predict, foreshadow, hold out
83 of nature = about nature ("learned men")
84 (1) beaten, devastated, tormented, (2) driven
85 resulting, following
86 falls off = parts company, withdraws, becomes estranged
87 break asunder, separate
88 revolts, rebellions
89 comes under = fits/falls into

against father. The King falls from bias[90] of nature: there's
105 father against child. We have seen the best of our time.[91]
Machinations,[92] hollowness, treachery, and all ruinous
disorders, follow us disquietly[93] to our graves. Find out[94] this
villain, Edmund, it shall lose[95] thee nothing, do it carefully.
And the noble and true-hearted Kent banished! His offense,
110 honesty! 'Tis strange.

EXIT GLOUCESTER

Edmund This is the excellent foppery of the world, that when
we are sick in fortune, often the surfeits[96] of our own
behavior, we make guilty of our disasters the sun, the moon,
and the stars, as if we were villains by necessity, fools by
115 heavenly compulsion, knaves, thieves, and treachers[97] by
spherical predominance,[98] drunkards, liars, and adulterers by
an enforced obedience of[99] planetary influence, and all that
we are evil in by[100] a divine thrusting[101] on. An admirable
evasion of[102] whoremaster man, to lay his goatish[103]
120 disposition to the charge[104] of a star! My father

90 the tendencies, inclinations, customary paths
91 age, era
92 plotting, scheming★
93 uneasily, uncomfortably
94 find out = unriddle, detect, discover
95 cost, deprive
96 often the surfeits = which are often the (1) faults, trespasses, (2) excesses
97 (1) cheaters, deceivers, (2) traitors
98 spherical predominance = superior strength/authority of the stars and
    planets ("spheres")
99 to
100 because of
101 pushing, driving
102 admirable evasion of = marvelous/wonderful/surprising escape by
103 lustful, lascivious
104 responsibility

compounded[105] with my mother under the Dragon's Tail,[106]
and my nativity was under Ursa Major,[107] so that it
follows[108] I am rough[109] and lecherous. Tut, I should have
been that[110] I am, had the maidenliest star in the firmament
twinkled on my bastardizing.   125

ENTER EDGAR

Pat![111] He comes like the catastrophe of[112] the old comedy.
My cue[113] is villainous melancholy, with a sigh like Tom o'
Bedlam.[114] O these eclipses do portend these divisions!
(*sings*) Fa, sol, la, mi.

Edgar   How now, brother Edmund, what serious   130
     contemplation are you in?

Edmund I am thinking, brother, of a prediction I read this other
     day, what should[115] follow these eclipses.

Edgar   Do you busy yourself with that?

Edmund I promise you, the effects he writes of succeed   135
     unhappily.[116] When saw you my father last?

Edgar   Why, the night gone by.

---

105 came together, joined
106 i.e., in Ptolemaic astronomy, the point at which the descending orbit of the
     moon intersects with the great circle formed by the meeting of the earth's
     orbit with the sphere in which the sun is located (Dragon's Tail: the
     appearance of the astrological chart representing this event)
107 Ursa Major = constellation known as the Great Bear
108 necessarily/inevitably happens that
109 coarse
110 would have been that = must have been what
111 and there he is!
112 catastrophe of = disasters that occur in
113 dramatic guide/hint
114 stock beggar/fool character★
115 is supposed to
116 succeed unhappily = follow unfortunately/unluckily/regrettably

Edmund Spake you with him?

Edgar Ay, two hours together.

140 *Edmund* Parted you in[117] good terms? Found you no displeasure in him, by word nor countenance?[118]

Edgar None at all.

Edmund Bethink[119] yourself wherein you may have offended him. And at my entreaty forbear his presence, till some little

145 time hath qualified[120] the heat of his displeasure, which at this instant so rageth in him, that with the[121] mischief of your person[122] it would scarcely allay.[123]

Edgar Some villain hath done me wrong.

Edmund That's my fear. I pray you, have a continent[124]

150 forbearance till the speed of his rage goes slower. And as I say, retire with me[125] to my lodging,[126] from whence I will fitly bring you to hear my lord speak. Pray ye go, there's my key. If you do stir abroad,[127] go armed.[128]

Edgar Armed, brother?

155 *Edmund* Brother, I advise you to[129] the best. I am no[130] honest

117 on
118 (1) behavior, gesture, attitude, (2) facial expression★
119 call to mind, recollect
120 modified
121 even with
122 mischief of your person = injury/harm ("evil") to your body
123 scarcely allay = hardly/barely be laid aside/abandoned
124 restrained, temperate
125 retire with me = withdraw/take shelter *in* my lodging, *not* together with me
126 bedroom (i.e., his lodging in his father's house, he not being a full-time resident therein)
127 stir abroad = out (of Edmund's room), at large, moving about★
128 i.e., carry a sword (firearms did not exist at the supposed date of this play)
129 for
130 am not an

man if there be any good meaning[131] toward you. I have told
you what I have seen, and heard. But faintly,[132] nothing like
the image[133] and horror of it. Pray you, away.[134]

Edgar   Shall I hear from you anon?[135]

Edmund I do[136] serve you in this business.   160

EXIT EDGAR

A credulous[137] father, and a brother noble,[138]
Whose nature is so far from doing harms[139]
That he suspects none. On whose foolish honesty
My practices[140] ride[141] easy. I see[142] the business.
Let me, if not by birth, have lands by wit.[143]   165
All with me's meet that I can fashion fit.

EXIT

131 intention
132 barely, feebly
133 (1) likeness, (2) vividly, graphically
134 leave, go★
135 shortly, quickly, soon
136 (an intensifier, of no syntactial significance)
137 over-ready to believe
138 of lofty/highly moral character
139 evil, mischief, hurt
140 (1) proceedings, operations, (2) schemes, machinations★
141 move, go, are carried (as is a man on horseback)
142 anticipate, foresee
143 intelligence ("mind")

SCENE 3

Albany's palace

<small>ENTER GONERIL, AND OSWALD, HER STEWARD</small>

Goneril Did my father strike my gentleman[1] for chiding of his
   Fool?[2]

Oswald Ay, madam.

Goneril By day and night he wrongs[3] me, every hour
   He flashes[4] into one gross crime[5] or other,
5   That sets us all at odds.[6] I'll not endure it.
   His knights grow riotous,[7] and himself upbraids us
   On[8] every trifle. When he returns from hunting,
   I will not speak with him, say I am sick.
   If you come slack of former[9] services,
10   You shall do well, the fault of it I'll answer.

Oswald He's coming, madam, I hear him.

<small>HUNTING HORNS WITHIN</small>

Goneril Put on[10] what weary negligence you please,
   You and your fellows.[11] I'll have it come to question.[12]

---

1 an attendant of good birth (as Oswald is not)
2 chiding of his Fool = scolding/reproving his professional jester/clown
3 deals unfairly/unjustly, injures
4 rushes, dashes, breaks out in
5 offense
6 all at odds = thoroughly at strife/variance
7 (1) difficult, troublesome, (2) wanton, dissolute, noisy★
8 about, on the occasion of
9 come slack of former = move toward a slackening/lessening★ of earlier
10 pretend, assume deceptively
11 co-workers
12 discussion

If he distaste[13] it, let him[14] to my sister,
Whose mind and mine I know in that are one,   15
Not to be overruled. Idle old man,
That still would manage those authorities[15]
That he hath given away! Now by my life,
Old fools are babes again, and must be used
With checks as[16] flatteries, when they are seen abused.[17]   20
Remember what I have said.

Oswald   Well,[18] madam.

Goneril And let his knights have[19] colder looks among you.
What grows of it, no matter, advise your fellows so. I'll write
straight[20] to my sister, to hold my course. Prepare for dinner.

EXEUNT

13 dislikes
14 let him = let him go
15 powers
16 just as with
17 used improperly/mistakenly/wrongly★ ("not to be overruled . . . seen
    abused": Quarto)
18 very well
19 receive, be given
20 immediately, without delay

SCENE 4

Albany's palace, a hall

ENTER KENT, DISGUISED

Kent If but as well[1] I other accents borrow,
    That can my speech defuse,[2] my good intent
    May carry through itself[3] to that full issue
    For which I razed[4] my likeness. Now banished Kent,
5   If thou canst serve where thou dost stand condemned,
    So may it come,[5] thy master whom thou lov'st,
    Shall find thee full of labors.

HORNS WITHIN

ENTER LEAR, KNIGHTS, AND ATTENDANTS

Lear Let me not stay a jot[6] for dinner, go get it ready.

EXIT AN ATTENDANT

    (*sees Kent*) How now, what art thou?
10   *Kent* A man, sir.

Lear What dost thou profess?[7] What wouldst thou with us?

Kent I do profess[8] to be no less than I seem, to serve him truly
    that will put me in trust,[9] to love him that is honest, to

---

1 i.e., if he can change his speech as successfully as he has his appearance
2 make indistinct
3 carry through itself = bring itself safely
4 (1) erased, obliterated, altered, (2) shaved
5 happen
6 stay a jot = delay the least bit
7 what dost thou profess = what is your trade/do you do
8 declare myself
9 put me in trust = trust/have confidence in me

converse with him that is wise and says little, to fear
judgment,[10] to fight when I cannot choose, and to eat no   15
fish.[11]

Lear What art thou?

Kent A very honest-hearted fellow, and as poor as the King.

Lear If thou be as poor for[12] a subject as he is for a king, thou
art poor enough. What wouldst thou?   20

Kent Service.[13]

Lear Who wouldst thou serve?

Kent You.

Lear Dost thou know me, fellow?[14]

Kent No sir, but you have that[15] in your countenance which I   25
would fain call master.

Lear What's that?

Kent Authority.

Lear What services canst thou do?

Kent I can keep honest counsel,[16] ride, run, mar a curious[17] tale   30
in telling it, and deliver[18] a plain message bluntly. That which
ordinary men are fit for, I am qualified in, and the best of me
is diligence.

Lear How old art thou?

10 divine punishment
11 (1) I am a Catholic, *or* (2) I am a meat-eater, *or* (3) I avoid whores, *or* (4) just
   see how funny I can be, ending with an irrelevancy like this (see note 17,
   below: "mar a curious tale")
12 poor for = deficient/inadequate as
13 domestic service
14 i.e., a form of address from a higher-status person to a lower-status one
15 that which, something
16 honest counsel = honorably keep secrets/confidences
17 mar a curious = spoil/ruin an ingenious/subtle/elaborate★
18 express, speak

35 *Kent*   Not so young sir, to love a woman for singing, nor so
old to dote[19] on her for anything. I have years on my back
forty-eight.

Lear   Follow me, thou shalt serve me. If I like thee no worse
after dinner, I will not part from thee yet. Dinner, ho,[20]
40 dinner! Where's my knave? My Fool? Go you, and call my
Fool hither.

EXIT AN ATTENDANT

ENTER OSWALD

You, you, sirrah, where's my daughter?

Oswald   So please you – [21]

EXIT OSWALD

Lear   What says the fellow there? Call the clotpoll[22] back.

EXIT AN ATTENDANT

45 Where's my Fool, ho? I think the world's asleep.

ATTENDANT RETURNS

How now? Where's that mongrel?

Attendant He says, my lord, your daughter is not well.

Lear   Why came not the slave[23] back to me when I called
him?

50 *Attendant* Sir, he answered me in the roundest[24] manner, he
would not.

19 foolishly bestow excessive love
20 hey!★
21 pardon/excuse me
22 blockhead, dolt
23 contemptuous word for a servant★
24 harshest, most summary/severe/brusque

Lear   He would not?

Attendant My lord, I know not what the matter is, but to my
     judgment, your Highness is not entertained[25] with that
     ceremonious affection as you were wont.[26] There's a great   55
     abatement[27] of kindness appears[28] as well in the general
     dependents,[29] as in the Duke himself also, and your daughter.

Lear   Ha? Sayest thou so?

Attendant I beseech you pardon me, my lord, if I be mistaken,
     for my duty cannot be silent when I think your Highness   60
     wronged.

Lear   Thou but rememberest[30] me of mine own
     conception.[31] I have perceived a most faint neglect of late,
     which I have rather blamed as mine own jealous[32] curiosity
     than as a very pretense[33] and purpose of unkindness. I will   65
     look further into't. But where's my Fool? I have not seen him
     this two days.

Attendant Since my young lady's[34] going into France, sir, the
     Fool hath much pined away.[35]

Lear   No more of that, I have noted[36] it well. Go you, and   70
     tell my daughter I would speak with her.

EXIT ATTENDANT

25 maintained, supported, received★
26 accustomed to★
27 lessening★
28 appearing, which appears
29 general dependents = all the subordinates/servants
30 reminds
31 notion, idea
32 suspicious, apprehensive, doubtful
33 very pretense = true assertion
34 Cordelia
35 pined away = languished, suffered, been troubled/distressed
36 perceived, noticed, marked★

Go you, call hither my Fool.

EXIT ATTENDANT

ENTER OSWALD

O you sir, you, come you hither, sir. Who am I, sir?

Oswald My lady's father.

75 *Lear* "My lady's father!" My lord's knave, you whoreson dog, you slave, you cur!

Oswald I am none of these, my lord, I beseech your pardon.

Lear Do you bandy[37] looks with me, you rascal?

LEAR STRIKES HIM

Oswald I'll not be strucken, my lord.

80 *Kent* Nor tripped neither, you base football[38] player.

KENT TRIPS OSWALD

Lear I thank thee, fellow. Thou servest me, and I'll love thee.

Kent (*to Oswald, yanking him upright*) Come, sir, arise, away, I'll teach you differences.[39] Away, away! If you will[40] measure your lubber's length[41] again, tarry. But away, go to.[42] Have

85 you wisdom?[43] So.

HE PUSHES OSWALD OUT

Lear Now, my friendly knave, I thank thee. There's earnest of[44] of thy service.

37 exchange, toss back and forth
38 rowdy form of soccer, played by boys
39 i.e., in rank/status
40 wish to
41 lubber's length = clumsy/stupid ("get knocked down")
42 go to = come, come
43 i.e., are you smart enough to get out of here
44 earnest of = (1) foretaste, (2) money for

HE GIVES KENT MONEY

ENTER FOOL

Fool Let me hire him too. (*to Kent*) Here's my coxcomb.[45]

Lear How now, my pretty[46] knave, how dost thou?

Fool Sirrah, you were best take my coxcomb.   90

Lear Why, my boy?

Fool Why, for taking one's part that's out of favor. Nay, an[47] thou
    canst not smile as the wind sits,[48] thou'lt catch cold shortly.
    There, take my coxcomb. Why, this fellow[49] has banished two
    on's[50] daughters, and did the third a blessing against his will. If   95
    thou follow him, thou must needs wear my coxcomb. (*to*
    Lear) How now, nuncle?[51] Would I had two coxcombs and
    two daughters.

Lear Why, my boy?

Fool If I gave them all my living,[52] I'ld keep my coxcombs   100
    myself. There's mine, beg another of thy daughters.

Lear Take heed sirrah, the whip.

Fool Truth's a dog must to kennel,[53] he must be whipped out,
    when[54] the Lady Brach[55] may stand by th' fire and stink.

Lear A pestilent gall[56] to me!   105

45 fool's cap
46 clever
47 if★
48 the way the wind blows (i.e., flatter those in power)
49 Lear
50 of his
51 uncle (dialectal variant)
52 income, way of life
53 (1) be returned to his kennel, (2) be kept quiet, shut up
54 out, when = away, while
55 bitch
56 pestilent gall = noxious/poisonous sore/exasperation/bitterness★

Fool Sirrah, I'll teach thee a speech.

Lear Do.

Fool Mark[57] it, nuncle.

Have more than thou showest,[58]

110 Speak less than thou knowest,

Lend less than thou owest,

Ride more than thou goest,[59]

Learn more than thou trowest,[60]

Set less than thou throwest.

115 Leave thy drink and thy whore,

And keep in-a-door,

And thou shalt have more

Than two tens to a score.[61]

Kent This is nothing, Fool.

120 *Fool* Then 'tis like the breath of an unfeed[62] lawyer, you gave me nothing for't. Can you make no use of nothing, nuncle?

Lear Why no, boy, nothing can be made out of nothing.

Fool (*to Kent*) Prithee, tell him, so much the rent[63] of his land comes to. He will not believe a fool.

125 *Lear* A bitter[64] fool!

Fool Dost thou know the difference, my boy, between a bitter fool and a sweet fool?

Lear No lad, teach me.

57 note, pay attention to★
58 display, exhibit★
59 walk
60 expect, believe
61 1 score = 20★
62 unpaid
63 revenue, income
64 disagreeable/hard/unpleasant (himself)

Fool[65]   That lord that counseled thee
            To give away thy land,   130
        Come place him here by me,
            Do thou for him stand.
        The sweet and bitter fool
            Will presently appear,
        The one[66] in motley[67] here,   135
            The other found out there.

Lear Dost thou call me fool, boy?

Fool All thy other titles thou hast given away. That thou wast
    born with.

Kent This is not altogether fool, my lord.   140

Fool Give me an egg, nuncle, and I'll give thee two crowns.

Lear What two crowns shall they be?

Fool Why, after I have cut the egg i' the middle, and eat[68] up the
    meat, the two crowns[69] of the egg. When thou clovest[70] thy
    crown i' the middle, and gavest away both parts, thou borest   145
    thy ass[71] on thy back o'er the dirt.[72] Thou hadst little wit in
    thy bald crown, when thou gavest thy golden one away. If I
    speak like myself[73] in this, let him be whipped that first finds
    it so.

HE SINGS

65 the next eleven lines are from Quarto
66 sweet one
67 fool's multicolored costume
68 ate (prounounced "et," in England, to this day)
69 rounded ends
70 split, cut
71 donkey (the human bottom in British English is "arse")
72 a popular fable: a man trying to please everyone ends up carrying his donkey
    on his back
73 i.e., like a fool

150　　　　Fools had ne'er less grace in a year,
　　　　　　　For wise men are grown foppish,
　　　　　　They know not how their wits to wear,[74]
　　　　　　　Their manners are so apish.[75]

　　　Lear When were you wont to be so full of songs, sirrah?
155 *Fool* I have used it,[76] nuncle, ever since thou madest thy
　　　　daughters thy mothers, for when thou gavest them the rod,
　　　　and put'st[77] down thine own breeches,

HE SINGS

　　　　　Then they for sudden joy did weep,
　　　　　　　And I for sorrow sung,
160　　　　That such a king should play bo-peep,[78]
　　　　　　　And go the fools among.

　　　　Prithee, nuncle, keep[79] a schoolmaster that can teach thy fool
　　　　to lie. I would fain learn to lie.

　　　Lear An you lie, sirrah, we'll have you whipped.
165 *Fool* I marvel what kin[80] thou and thy daughters are. They'll
　　　　have me whipped for speaking true, thou'lt have me whipped
　　　　for lying, and sometimes I am whipped for holding my peace.
　　　　I had rather be any kind o' thing than a Fool, and yet I would
　　　　not be thee, nuncle. Thou hast pared[81] thy wit o' both sides,
170　　　and left nothing i' the middle. Here comes one o' the parings.

74 use, employ
75 ape-like, silly
76 used it = been in the habit of it
77 pulled
78 i.e., be childish
79 employ
80 what kin = how birth-related
81 trimmed by cutting

ENTER GONERIL

Lear   How now, daughter? What makes that frontlet[82] on?[83]
Methinks you are too much of late i' the frown.[84]

Fool   Thou wast a pretty fellow when thou hadst no need to
care for her frowning. Now thou art an O[85] without a
figure.[86] I am better than thou art now. I am a Fool, thou art   175
nothing. (*to Goneril*) Yes, forsooth,[87] I will hold my tongue.
So your face bids me, though you say nothing.

  Mum, mum,

  He that keeps nor crust nor crumb,

  Weary of all, shall want some.   180

(*pointing to Lear*) That's a shealed peascod.[88]

Goneril   Not only, sir, this your all-licensed[89] Fool,
But other of your insolent[90] retinue
Do hourly carp and quarrel,[91] breaking forth
In rank[92] (and not to be endured) riots, sir.   185
I had thought, by making this well known unto you,
To have found a safe redress,[93] but now grow fearful,
By what yourself too late have spoke and done,

---

82 literally, bandage worn at night, to prevent/remove wrinkles; here, a frown,
  wrinkling up the forehead like a frontlet
83 what makes that frontlet on? = why are you wearing that frown-bandage?
84 i' the frown = in the habit of frowning
85 (1) circle, (2) zero
86 (1) picture, (2) face
87 truly
88 shealed pescod = shelled pea pod
89 all-licensed = all-permitted/tolerated/privileged
90 haughty, overbearing
91 carp and quarrel = chatter and complain
92 violent, gross
93 relief, remedy

That you protect this course, and put it on[94]
190   By your allowance[95] – which if you should, the fault
Would not 'scape censure, nor the redresses sleep,
Which in the tender[96] of a wholesome weal,[97]
Might in their working[98] do you that offense,
Which else were[99] shame, that[100] then necessity
Will call[101] discreet proceeding.

195 *Fool*   For you know, nuncle,
          The hedge-sparrow fed the cuckoo so long
          That it's had it[102] head bit off by it young.[103]
      So out went the candle, and we were left darkling.[104]

      Lear   Are you our daughter?

200 *Goneril* Come, sir,
      I would you would make use of that good wisdom
      (Whereof I know you are fraught)[105] and put away
      These dispositions,[106] which of late transport[107] you
      From what you rightly are.

205 *Fool*   May not an ass know when the cart draws the horse?
      Whoop, Jug![108] I love thee.

      94 encourage/incite it
      95 approval, acceptance, permission★
      96 (?) texture? working? urge toward?
      97 wholesome weal = healthy social fabric ("general good")
      98 their working = the operation of the censures and redresses
      99 else were = otherwise would be
      100 but that
      101 name, identify as
      102 its
      103 it young = the cuckoo's much larger chick
      104 in darkness
      105 filled, supplied, equipped
      106 inclinations
      107 remove, carry away
      108 Joan (spoken to Goneril?)

Lear　Doth any[109] here know me? This is not Lear.
　　Doth Lear walk thus? Speak thus? Where are his eyes?
　　Either his notion[110] weakens, his discernings[111]
　　Are lethargied.[112] Ha! Waking? 'Tis not so.　　　　　　210
　　Who is it that can tell me who I am?

Fool　Lear's shadow.

Lear　Your name, fair gentlewoman?

Goneril　This admiration,[113] sir, is much o' the savor[114]
　　Of other[115] your new pranks. I do beseech you　　　　215
　　To understand my purposes aright.
　　As you are old and reverend, should[116] be wise.
　　Here do you keep a hundred knights and squires,
　　Men so disordered,[117] so deboshed[118] and bold,
　　That this our court,[119] infected with their manners,　　220
　　Shows[120] like a riotous inn. Epicurism[121] and lust
　　Make it more like a tavern or a brothel
　　Than a gracèd palace. The shame itself doth speak
　　For instant remedy. Be then desired
　　By her, that else will take the thing she begs,　　　　225

109 anyone
110 mind
111 perceptions
112 afflicted by morbid drowsiness
113 astonishment, surprise, wondering
114 taste, flavoring
115 other of
116 you should
117 disorderly*
118 debauched
119 courtyard
120 seems, looks
121 sensuality, the pursuit of pleasure

A little to disquantity your train,[122]

And the remainder that shall still depend,[123]

To be such men as may besort[124] your age,

And know themselves and you.

Lear   Darkness and devils!

230 Saddle my horses, call my train together.

Degenerate bastard! I'll not trouble thee.

Yet[125] have I left a daughter.

Goneril You strike my people, and your disordered rabble[126]

Make servants of their betters.

ENTER ALBANY

235 *Lear*   Woe, that too late repents – (*To Albany*) O sir, are you come?

Is it your will? Speak, sir. Prepare my horses.

Ingratitude, thou marble-hearted fiend,

More hideous when thou show'st thee[127] in a child

Than the sea-monster!

Albany   Pray, sir, be patient.

240 *Lear*   (*to Goneril*) Detested kite,[128] thou liest.

My train are men of choice and rarest parts,[129]

That all particulars of duty[130] know,

---

122 disquantity your train = diminish/lessen your retinue, following, attendants★

123 be maintained

124 match, befit

125 still

126 mob

127 show'st thee = show yourself (i.e., ingratitude)

128 bird of prey, hawk

129 qualities, capabilities

130 particulars of duty = details/elements of the required actions of personal service

And in the most exact regard support[131]
The worships[132] of their name.[133] O most small fault,
How ugly didst thou in Cordelia show![134]   245
Which[135] like an engine[136] wrenched my frame of nature[137]
From the fixed place, drew from my heart all love,
And added to the gall. (*striking his head*) O Lear, Lear, Lear!
Beat at this gate that let thy folly in
And thy dear judgment out! Go, go,[138] my people.   250

EXIT KENT, ATTENDANTS

Albany My lord, I am guiltless, as I am ignorant
    Of what hath moved[139] you.

Lear   It may be so, my lord.
    Hear Nature, hear dear goddess, hear!
    Suspend thy purpose, if thou didst intend
    To make this creature fruitful!   255
    Into her womb convey sterility,
    Dry up in her the organs of increase,[140]
    And from her derogate[141] body never spring
    A babe to honor her! If she must teem,[142]

131 regard support = uphold all aspect/circumstances
132 honor, dignity
133 reputation, rank
134 appear
135 i.e., the "small fault" looked far bigger to him, and had the disastrous results
      he proceeds to record
136 a battering ram, or some such mechanical contrivance
137 frame of nature = natural/normal disposition/state ("structure of being")
138 go, go = leave, leave
139 disturbed, provoked, excited
140 propagation, reproduction
141 debased
142 bring forth

260   Create her child of spleen,[143] that it may live
        And be a thwart disnatured[144] torment to her!
        Let it stamp wrinkles in her brow of youth,
        With cadent[145] tears fret channels[146] in her cheeks,
        Turn all her mother's pains and benefits[147]
265   To laughter and contempt, that she may feel
        How sharper than a serpent's tooth it is
        To have a thankless child! Away, away!

EXIT LEAR

Albany   Now gods that we adore, whereof comes this?
Goneril   Never afflict[148] yourself to know more of it,
270   But let his disposition have that scope
        That dotage gives it.

ENTER LEAR

Lear   What, fifty of my followers at a clap?[149]
        Within a fortnight?[150]
Albany   What's the matter, sir?
Lear   I'll tell thee. (*to Goneril*) Life and death, I am ashamed
275   That thou hast power to shake my manhood thus,
        That these hot tears, which break from me perforce,[151]
        Should make thee worth them. Blasts and fogs upon thee!

143   of spleen = out of/from peevishness/bad temper
144   thwart disnatured = perverse/cross-grained unnatural
145   dripping
146   fret channels = chafe/rub/gnaw/wear grooves/furrows
147   pains and benefits = efforts/care and kindness
148   never afflict = don't ever distress/grieve
149   stroke
150   two weeks
151   of necessity, by compulsion★

Th' untented woundings[152] of a father's curse
Pierce[153] every sense about thee! (*to himself*) Old fond eyes,
Beweep this cause[154] again, I'll pluck ye out,   280
And cast you, with the waters that you loose,
To temper clay.[155] Ha? Let it be so.
I have another daughter,
Who I am sure is kind and comfortable.[156]
When she shall hear this of thee, with her nails   285
She'll flay[157] thy wolfish visage. Thou shalt find
That I'll resume the shape which thou dost think
I have cast off for ever.

EXEUNT LEAR, KENT, AND ATTENDANTS

Goneril   Do you mark that?
Albany I cannot be so partial, Goneril,
   To[158] the great love I bear you –   290
Goneril Pray you, content.[159] What Oswald, ho!
   (*to Fool*) You sir, more knave than fool, after[160] your master.
Fool   Nuncle Lear, nuncle Lear, tarry; take the Fool with thee.
   A fox, when one has caught her,
      And such a daughter,   295
      Should sure to the slaughter,

---

152 untented woundings = exposed / open wounds
153 (1) penetrate, (2) deeply wound / affect / move★
154 beweep this cause = if you weep for this action
155 temper clay = mix
156 supporting, comforting
157 strip the skin off
158 partial . . . to = influenced / biased by
159 stop complaining ('be quiet')
160 go after / behind

If my cap would buy a halter.[161]
So the Fool follows after.

EXIT FOOL

Goneril This man[162] hath had good counsel.[163] A hundred
knights?

300 'Tis politic[164] and safe to let him keep
At point[165] a hundred knights! Yes, that[166] on every dream,
Each buzz, each fancy,[167] each complaint, dislike,
He may enguard[168] his dotage with their powers,
And hold our lives in mercy. Oswald, I say!

305 *Albany* Well, you may fear too far.

Goneril Safer than trust too far:
Let me still[169] take away the harms I fear,
Not fear still to be taken.[170] I know his heart.
What he hath uttered I have writ my sister.

310 If she sustain him and his hundred knights
When I have showed the unfitness –

ENTER OSWALD

How now, Oswald?
What, have you writ that letter to my sister?

161 rope, strap
162 Lear
163 advice
164 prudent, wise
165 ready, fully prepared ("armed")
166 so that
167 each buzz, each fancy = each whim, each delusive imagining
168 protect
169 always
170 seized, captured (by them)★

Oswald Yes, madam.

Goneril Take you some company,[171] and away to horse.

    Inform her full of my particular[172] fear,   315

    And thereto add such reasons of your own

    As may compact[173] it more. Get you gone,

    And hasten your return.

EXIT OSWALD

                No, no, my lord,

    This milky gentleness and course of yours

    Though I condemn not, yet under pardon,[174]   320

    You are much more at task[175] for want of wisdom

    Than praised for harmful mildness.

Albany How far your eyes may pierce I cannot tell.

    Striving to better, oft we mar what's well.

Goneril Nay, then –

Albany   Well, well, th' event.   325

EXEUNT

---

171 other servants ("escort")
172 (1) private, (2) special
173 tighten, make firmer
174 under pardon = excuse me, if you don't mind my saying
175 at task = to be blamed

SCENE 5

Courtyard of Albany's palace

enter Lear, Kent, and Fool

Lear (*to Kent*) Go you before[1] to Gloucester with these letters. Acquaint my daughter no further with anything you know than comes from her demand out of[2] the letter. If your diligence[3] be not speedy, I shall be there afore you.

5   *Kent* I will not sleep, my lord, till I have delivered your letter.

exit Kent

Fool If a man's brains were in's heels, were't not[4] in danger of kibes?[5]

Lear Ay, boy.

Fool Then, I prithee, be merry, thy wit shall ne'er go slip-shod.[6]

10   *Lear* Ha, ha, ha!

Fool Shalt[7] see thy other daughter will use thee kindly, for though she's as like this as a crab's[8] like an apple, yet I can tell what I can tell.

Lear Why, what canst thou tell, my boy?

15   *Fool* She will taste as like this[9] as a crab does to a crab. Thou canst tell why one's nose stands i'the middle on's[10] face?

1 ahead of me
2 demand out of = request because of (i.e., only "after she reads")
3 effort, exertion
4 were't not = would the mind/brains not be
5 chilblains (swelling/inflammation, caused by cold)
6 slip-shod = wearing slippers/loose shoes
7 you will
8 crab apple
9 Goneril
10 on his

Lear No.

Fool Why, to keep one's eyes of[11] either side's nose. That what a
man cannot smell out, he may spy into.

Lear I did her wrong.   20

Fool Canst tell how an oyster makes his shell?

Lear No.

Fool Nor I neither. But I can tell why a snail has a house.

Lear Why?

Fool Why, to put his head in, not to give it away to his   25
daughters, and leave his horns without a case.[12]

Lear I will forget my nature.[13] So kind a father! Be my horses
ready?

Fool Thy asses[14] are gone about[15] 'em. The reason why the
seven stars are no more than seven is a pretty reason.   30

Lear Because they are not eight?

Fool Yes, indeed. Thou wouldst make a good Fool.

Lear To take't again perforce![16] Monster[17] ingratitude!

Fool If thou wert my Fool, nuncle, I'ld have thee beaten for
being old before thy time.   35

Lear How's that?

Fool Thou shouldst not have been old till thou hadst been wise.

Lear O, let me not be mad, not mad, sweet heaven.
Keep me in temper.[18] I would not[19] be mad!

11 on
12 receptacle, covering, sheath, box
13 natural disposition
14 i.e., Lear's attendants
15 to see about
16 take't again perforce = take it back by force / violence
17 (adjective) monstrous
18 balance, good adjustment
19 would not = do not want to

ENTER ATTENDANT

40   How now, are the horses ready?
Attendant Ready, my lord.
Lear   Come, boy.

EXEUNT LEAR AND ATTENDANT

Fool   She that's a maid[20] now, and[21] laughs at my
    departure[22]
    Shall not be a maid long, unless things[23] be cut shorter.

EXIT

20 virgin
21 (?) if she
22 i.e., on such a fool's errand
23 penises

Act 2

🛡

SCENE I

Gloucester's castle

ENTER EDMUND AND CURRAN, FROM OPPOSITE
SIDES OF THE STAGE

Edmund Save thee,[1] Curran.

Curran And you, sir. I have been with your father, and given
him notice that the Duke of Cornwall, and Regan his
Duchess, will be here with him this night.

Edmund How comes that?   5

Curran Nay, I know not. You have heard of the news abroad,
I mean the whispered ones,[2] for they are yet but ear-kissing
arguments?[3]

Edmund Not I. Pray you, what are they?

Curran Have you heard of no likely wars toward,[4] 'twixt the   10
Dukes of Cornwall and Albany?

---

1 save you = may God save you (a conventional greeting)
2 "news" was a plural
3 ear-kissing arguments = whispered statements / claims
4 coming, approaching★ (taWARD)

Edmund Not a word.

Curran You may do then, in time. Fare you well, sir.

EXIT CURRAN

Edmund The Duke be here tonight? The better – best!
15   This weaves itself perforce into my business.
My father hath set guard to take[5] my brother,
And I have one thing, of a queasy question,[6]
Which I must act.[7] Briefness[8] and fortune, work!
Brother, a word, descend! Brother, I say!

ENTER EDGAR

20   My father watches. O sir, fly this place,
Intelligence is given[9] where you are hid.
You have now the good advantage[10] of the night.
Have you not spoken 'gainst the Duke of Cornwall?
He's coming hither, now i' the night, i' the haste,
25   And Regan with him. Have you nothing said
Upon his party[11] 'gainst the Duke of Albany?
Advise yourself.[12]

Edgar   I am sure on't,[13] not a word.

Edmund I hear my father coming. Pardon me,
In cunning[14] I must draw my sword upon you.

---

5 set guard to take = arranged for armed men to capture
6 queasy question = ticklish/uncertain/delicate inquiry/investigation
7 put in motion, perform, carry out
8 brevity/quickness
9 intelligence is given = knowledge has been delivered
10 good advantage = useful gain/profit
11 dispute, affair
12 advise yourself = consider, think about it
13 on't = on it = of/about it
14 cleverness, ingenuity

Draw, seem to defend yourself. Now quit[15] you well.   30
Yield, come before my father. Light ho, here!
Fly, brother. Torches, torches! (*to Edgar*) So farewell.

EXIT EDGAR

Some blood drawn on me would beget opinion[16]
Of my more fierce endeavor.

HE WOUNDS HIS ARM

                        I have seen drunkards
Do more than this in sport. Father, father!   35
Stop, stop! No help?

ENTER GLOUCESTER, AND SERVANTS WITH TORCHES

Gloucester   Now Edmund, where's the villain?
Edmund   Here stood he in the dark, his sharp sword out,
    Mumbling of[17] wicked charms, conjuring the moon
    To stand auspicious mistress[18] –
Gloucester   But where is he?[19]   40
Edmund   Look, sir, I bleed.
Gloucester   Where is the villain, Edmund?[20]
Edmund   Fled this way, sir. When by no means he could –
Gloucester   Pursue him, ho, go after!

EXEUNT SOME SERVANTS

15 acquit, prove ("do/play your part")
16 beget opinion = create belief
17 mumbling of = muttering
18 stand auspicious mistress = become a favorable/kind goddess/governor
    ("person in power/control")
19 but WHERE is HE
20 where IS the VILlain EDmund

                      By no means what?

Edmund Persuade me to the murder of your lordship.

45   But[21] that I told him the revenging gods

      'Gainst parricides[22] did all their thunders[23] bend –

      Spoke with how manifold and strong a bond

      The child was bound to th' father – sir, in fine,[24]

      Seeing how loathly opposite[25] I stood

50   To his unnatural purpose, in fell motion,[26]

      With his preparèd[27] sword, he charges home[28]

      My unprovided[29] body, latched[30] mine arm.

      But when he saw my best alarumed[31] spirits,

      Bold in the quarrel's right,[32] roused to the encounter,

55   Or whether gasted[33] by the noise[34] I made,

      Full suddenly he fled.

Gloucester   Let him fly far.

      Not in this land shall he remain uncaught

      And found. (*to servants*) Dispatch![35] The noble Duke my

      master,[36]

21 except

22 those who murder their fathers

23 thunders bend = lightning bolts hurl down/aim

24 in fine = in short

25 loathly opposite = abhorrently/dreadfully opposed

26 fell motion = fierce/ruthless/cruel movement ("thrust")

27 readied

28 toward, at

29 unequipped ("not armored")

30 struck

31 alarumed = aroused

32 quarrel's right = my rectitude/righteousness in the dispute

33 frightened, alarmed

34 outcry, clamor

35 (1) hurry, (2) settle/take care of this

36 commander, leader, governor

My worthy arch and patron,[37] comes tonight.
By his authority I will proclaim[38] it,   60
That[39] he which finds him shall deserve our thanks,
Bringing the murderous coward to the stake,[40]
He that conceals him: death.
Edmund When I dissuaded him[41] from his intent,
And found him pight[42] to do it, with curst[43] speech   65
I threatened to discover[44] him. He replied,
"Thou unpossessing[45] bastard! Dost thou think,
If I would stand against[46] thee, would the reposal[47]
Of any trust, virtue, or worth in thee
Make thy words faithed?[48] No, what I should deny   70
(As this I would, though thou didst produce[49]
My very character), I'ld turn[50] it all
To thy suggestion, plot, and damnèd practice.
And thou must make a dullard of the world,
If they not thought the profits of[51] my death   75
Were very pregnant[52] and potential spurs

37 arch and patron = chief/superior and lord/protector
38 officially announce★
39 so that
40 the stake = execution
41 dissuaded him = advised/exhorted against
42 set, determined (PITE)
43 harsh, fierce, irritated
44 expose, reveal ("betray")
45 penniless ("owning nothing")
46 stand against = oppose
47 placing, reliance
48 believed
49 represent, exhibit
50 bend, twist, change
51 from
52 weighty, convincing, obvious

To make thee seek it."

Gloucester   O strange and fastened[53] villain,
Would he deny his letter? Said he?[54]

TUCKET[55] WITHIN

Hark, the Duke's trumpets. I know not why he comes.
80   All ports I'll bar, the villain shall not 'scape.
The Duke must grant me that. Besides, his picture[56]
I will send far and near, that all the kingdom
May have due note[57] of him. And of my land,
Loyal and natural[58] boy, I'll work[59] the means
85   To make thee capable.[60]

ENTER CORNWALL, REGAN, AND ATTENDANTS

Cornwall   How now, my noble friend. Since I came hither,
Which I can call but[61] now, I have heard strange news.
Regan   If it be true, all vengeance comes too short
Which can pursue the offender. How dost,[62] my lord?
90   *Gloucester*   O, madam, my old heart is cracked, it's cracked.
Regan   What, did my father's godson seek your life?
He whom my father named, your Edgar?
Gloucester   O, lady, lady, shame would have it[63] hid.

53 confirmed, settled
54 said he = did he say that
55 trumpet flourish
56 description
57 due note = proper/sufficient notice
58 illegitimate
59 manage, create, make ("arrange")
60 able (to inherit Gloucester's lands)
61 call but = say was just
62 are you
63 would have it = wishes it to be

Regan   Was he not companion with the riotous knights

That tended[64] upon my father?   95

Gloucester I know not, madam. 'Tis too bad, too bad.

Edmund   Yes, madam, he was of that consort.[65]

Regan   No marvel then, though he were ill affected.[66]

'Tis they have put him on[67] the old man's death,

To have th' expense[68] and waste of his revenues.   100

I have this present[69] evening from my sister

Been well informed of them, and with such cautions

That if they come to sojourn at my house,

I'll not be there.

Cornwall   Nor I, assure thee, Regan.

Edmund, I hear that you have shown your father   105

A child-like office.[70]

Edmund   'Twas my duty, sir.

Gloucester He did bewray his practice,[71] and received

This hurt[72] you see, striving to apprehend him.

Cornwall   Is he pursued?

Gloucester   Ay, my good lord.

Cornwall   If he be taken, he shall never more   110

Be feared of doing[73] harm. Make your own purpose,[74]

---

64 waited ("served")★

65 company ("crowd")

66 though he were ill affected = even supposing he was previously/already
   badly disposed/inclined

67 put him on = incite/encourage/urge him

68 spending, disbursement

69 very, same

70 child-like office = filial service/duty★

71 he did bewray his practice = Edmund exposed Edgar's

72 wound★

73 feared of doing = feared for the doing of

74 intention, determination

How[75] in my strength[76] you please. For you, Edmund,
Whose virtue and obedience doth this instant
So much commend[77] itself, you shall be ours.
115   Natures of such deep trust we shall much need.
You we first seize on.

Edmund   I shall serve you sir
Truly, however else.[78]

Gloucester   For him[79] I thank your Grace.

Cornwall   You know not why we came to visit you?

Regan   Thus out of season,[80] threading[81] dark-eyed night,
120   Occasions,[82] noble Gloucester, of some prize[83]
Wherein we must have use of your advice.
Our father he hath writ, so hath our sister,
Of differences,[84] which I best thought it fit
To answer from[85] our home. The several messengers
125   From hence attend dispatch.[86] Our good old friend,
Lay comforts[87] to your bosom, and bestow
Your needful counsel to our business,

75 however
76 authority, power
77 recommend
78 i.e., however effective I may be
79 for him = on his behalf
80 thus out of season = our coming like this, so inappropriately/
    inconveniently
81 making our way through
82 is induced/caused
83 contest
84 disputes, quarrels
85 while we are away from
86 attend dispatch = are waiting to be sent
87 lay comforts = set/place encouragement/strength/refreshment ("brace
    yourself")

Which craves the instant use.[88]
Gloucester   I serve you, madam.
Your Graces are right welcome.

EXEUNT

88 instant use = urgent/immediate utilization/employment (of your advice)

SCENE 2

In front of Gloucester's castle

Oswald Good dawning[1] to thee, friend. Art of this house?[2]

Kent Ay.

Oswald Where may we set[3] our horses?

Kent I' the mire.[4]

5 *Oswald* Prithee, if thou lovest me, tell me.

Kent I love thee not.

Oswald Why then, I care not for[5] thee.

Kent If I had thee in Lipsbury pinfold,[6] I would make thee
care for me.

10 *Oswald* Why dost thou use me thus? I know thee not.

Kent Fellow, I know thee.

Oswald What dost thou know me for?[7]

Kent A knave, a rascal, an eater of broken meats,[8] a base,
proud, shallow, beggarly,[9] three-suited,[10] hundred-pound,[11]

15 filthy, worsted-stocking[12] knave, a lily-livered, action-taking[13]

1 daybreak (i.e., when it comes, before too long: it is still night)
2 household
3 put
4 (1) mud, (2) bog
5 care not for = have no interest in
6 pound for stray animals
7 as, as representing
8 broken meats = leftover bits of food/drink
9 worthless
10 i.e., "service" included clothing; this would be Oswald's clothing allotment
11 i.e., salary per year
12 worsted = wool (servants wore wool stockings)
13 i.e., preferring litigation ("action") to fighting

knave, whoreson, glass-gazing, super-serviceable[14] finical[15]
rogue, one-trunk-inheriting[16] slave, one that wouldst be a
bawd, in way of good service, and art nothing but the
composition[17] of a knave, beggar, coward, pander,[18] and the
son and heir of a mongrel bitch – one whom I will beat into   20
clamorous whining, if thou deniest the least syllable of thy
addition.[19]

Oswald   Why, what a monstrous fellow art thou, thus to rail on[20]
one that is neither known of thee nor knows thee!

Kent   What a brazen-faced varlet[21] art thou, to deny thou   25
knowest me! Is it two days ago since I tripped up thy heels,
and beat thee before the King? Draw,[22] you rogue, for though
it be night, yet the moon shines. I'll make a sop[23] o' the
moonshine of[24] you. Draw, you whoreson cullionly[25]
barber-monger,[26] draw.   30

KENT DRAWS HIS SWORD

Oswald   Away, I have nothing to do with thee.[27]

---

14 ready to serve
15 fussy, affectedly fastidious
16 i.e., having no family able to leave him more than what a single trunk can
    hold
17 combination
18 pimp
19 description, title
20 rail on = abuse*
21 brazen-faced varlet = impudent rogue / rascal / menial
22 draw your sword
23 something dunked in soup (usually bread)
24 out of
25 despicable, base (cullion: testicle)
26 fop (one who is always seen in barbers' shops)
27 i.e., gentlemen (which Oswald is not) do not dirty their swords on wretches
    like you

Kent   Draw, you rascal. You come with letters against the
         King, and take Vanity[28] the puppet's[29] part against the royalty
         of her father. Draw, you rogue, or I'll so[30] carbonado[31] your
35   shanks.[32] Draw, you rascal, come your ways.[33]
Oswald   Help, ho, murder, help!
Kent   Strike,[34] you slave. Stand,[35] rogue, stand. You neat[36]
         slave, strike.

KENT BEATS HIM

Oswald   Help, ho, murder, murder!

ENTER EDMUND (SWORD DRAWN), CORNWALL,
REGAN, GLOUCESTER, AND SERVANTS

40 *Edmund*   How now, what's the matter? Part![37]
    Kent   With[38] you, goodman[39] boy, an you please. Come, I'll
             flesh[40] ye, come on, young master.
    Gloucester Weapons? Arms?[41] What's the matter here?
    Cornwall Keep peace,[42] upon your lives.

---

28 i.e., like a character in the old morality plays
29 (1) Vanity as a puppet, (2) "puppet" as contemptuous term for a woman,
   Oswald being a follower of Goneril
30 like this
31 slash, hack
32 legs (from knee to ankle)
33 come your ways = come on, do the right thing
34 swing your sword
35 fight back, stay where you are
36 unmitigated, absolute, complete
37 separate ("break it up")
38 I'll fight with
39 used only with men lower in rank than gentlemen (i.e., insulting, as of
   course so is "boy")
40 stick, pierce
41 fighting
42 order! stop!

He dies that strikes again. What is the matter? 45

Regan   The messengers[43] from our sister and the King.

Cornwall What is your difference? Speak.

Oswald   I am scarce in breath, my lord.

Kent   No marvel, you have so bestirred[44] your valor. You
cowardly rascal, Nature disclaims in thee. A tailor made 50
thee.[45]

Cornwall Thou art a strange fellow: a tailor make a man?

Kent   Ay, a tailor, sir. A stonecutter or painter could not have
made him so ill, though he had been but two hours at the
trade. 55

Cornwall Speak yet,[46] how grew your quarrel?

Oswald   This ancient ruffian, sir, whose life I have spared at suit
of[47] his gray beard –

Kent   Thou whoreson zed,[48] thou unnecessary letter![49] My
lord, if you will give me leave,[50] I will tread[51] this unbolted 60
villain[52] into mortar,[53] and daub the wall of a jakes[54] with
him. Spare my gray beard, you wagtail?[55]

Cornwall Peace sirrah!

---

43 i.e, Oswald and those with him
44 displayed
45 i.e., you're just clothing, all on the outside and nothing within
46 speak yet = continue, go on
47 at suit of = at the entreaty (i.e., because/in consideration of)
48 letter Z
49 i.e., spelling could manage with the letter S
50 permission★
51 trample, crush
52 unbolted villain = unsifted (i.e., not yet truly examined/tested) low-born
peasant★
53 powder (literally, masonry cement)
54 privy, outhouse
55 contemptible fellow (literally, a small bird with a constantly wagging tail)

You beastly[56] knave, know you no reverence?

65 *Kent*   Yes sir, but anger hath a privilege.[57]

Cornwall Why art thou angry?

Kent   That such a slave as this should wear a sword,

Who wears[58] no honesty. Such smiling rogues as these,

Like rats, oft bite the holy cords[59] atwain,[60]

70 Which are too intrinse t'unloose,[61] smooth[62] every passion

That in the natures of their lords rebel,[63]

Being oil to fire, snow to their colder moods,

Renege,[64] affirm, and turn their halcyon[65] beaks

With every gall and vary[66] of their masters,

75 Knowing nought (like dogs) but following.[67]

(*to Oswald*) A plague upon your epileptic[68] visage!

Smile you my[69] speeches, as[70] I were a fool?

Goose, if I had you upon Sarum[71] plain,

I'ld drive ye cackling home to Camelot.[72]

---

56 brutish ("animal-like")

57 right, exemption, immunity, license

58 employs, uses

59 holy cords = sacred/venerable ties/threads/bonds (of society, family, etc.)

60 apart, in two (aTWEN)

61 intrinse t'unloose = intricate/entangled to untie/slacken

62 make the way easy for

63 (verb) rise up, are disobedient

64 deny, abandon, renounce

65 calm (after the legendary halcyon bird, which soothed the sea's rough winds and waves) (HALseeON)

66 gall and vary = irritation/exasperation and hesitation/vacillation/variance

67 but following = except how to be a follower/servant

68 i.e., spasmodic, twitching

69 at my

70 as if

71 Salisbury (SALZbaREE)

72 (?)

Cornwall   What, art thou mad, old fellow?   80

Gloucester How fell you out?[73] Say that.

Kent   No contraries[74] hold more antipathy[75]

    Than I and such a knave.

Cornwall   Why dost thou call him a knave? What's his offense?

Kent   His countenance likes me not.[76]   85

Cornwall   No more, perchance,[77] does mine, nor his, nor hers.

Kent   Sir, 'tis my occupation[78] to be plain.

    I have seen better faces in my time

    Than stands on any shoulder that I see

    Before me at this instant.

Cornwall   This is some fellow,   90

    Who having been praised for bluntness, doth affect

    A saucy roughness, and constrains the garb[79]

    Quite from his nature.[80] He cannot flatter, he,

    An honest mind and plain, he must speak truth.

    An they will take it, so. If not, he's plain.   95

    These kind of knaves I know, which in this plainness

    Harbor more craft[81] and more corrupter ends[82]

    Than twenty silly-ducking observants[83]

73 fell you out = did you disagree / quarrel
74 opposites
75 natural incompatibility (anTIpaTHEE)
76 likes me not = I don't like
77 perhaps, maybe
78 habit, custom
79 constrains the garb = forces his behavior
80 quite from his nature = entirely naturally
81 cunning, art
82 devices, purposes
83 silly-ducking observants = head-bowing (like ducks in water) attendants / followers / servants

That stretch their duties nicely.[84]

100 *Kent*   Sir, in good sooth,[85] in sincere verity,

Under th' allowance of your great aspect,[86]

Whose influence,[87] like the wreath[88] of radiant fire

On flickering Phoebus' front[89] –

Cornwall   What mean'st by this?

Kent   To go out of my dialect,[90] which you discommend[91]

105 so much. I know, sir, I am no flatterer. He that beguiled[92] you

in a plain accent was a plain knave, which for my part I will

not be, though I should win your displeasure to entreat me

to't.[93]

Cornwall (*to Oswald*) What was the offense you gave him?

110 *Oswald*   I never gave him any.

It pleased the King his master very late

To strike at me, upon his misconstruction,[94]

When he,[95] conjunct[96] and flattering his[97] displeasure,

Tripped me behind. Being[98] down, insulted,[99] railed,

---

84 stretch their duties nicely = work/labor hard/strain at their foolish/dainty
jobs/homage/deference

85 truth

86 astrological position

87 astrological power

88 coil

89 flickering Phoebus' front = the wavering rays that appear on the sun's face

90 regional way of speech

91 disapprove of

92 he that beguiled = he who deceived★

93 win your displeasure to entreat me to't = (?) talk you/your angry self into
asking me to be a plain knave

94 i.e., the King misunderstood what I had said

95 Kent

96 associating himself with

97 the King's

98 I being

99 he insulted

And put upon him[100] such a deal of man,[101]   115
That[102] worthied[103] him, got praises of[104] the King
For him attempting[105] who[106] was self-subdued,
And in the fleshment[107] of this dread[108] exploit,
Drew on me here again.

Kent   None of these rogues and cowards   120
But[109] Ajax is their fool.[110]

Cornwall   Fetch forth the stocks![111]
You stubborn ancient knave, you reverend[112] braggart,
We'll teach you.

Kent   Sir, I am too old to learn.
Call not your[113] stocks for me. I serve the King,
On whose employment I was sent to you.   125
You shall do small respect, show too bold malice[114]
Against the grace and person of my master,
Stocking[115] his messenger.

Cornwall Fetch forth the stocks! As I have life and honor,

---

100 put upon him = assumed, adopted
101 deal of man = quantity/amount ("lot") of masculinity
102 which pretense of masculine prowess
103 made him seem honored
104 from
105 him attempting = his (Kent) attacking
106 he who (Oswald)
107 excitement
108 (sarcastic)
109 none of these . . . but = all of these
110 Ajax is their fool = make fun/are contemptuous of the irascible but brave
    Greek warrior Ajax
111 penal device, in which the victim was locked (feet and sometimes hands)
    between two notched planks
112 old
113 the
114 (1) ill-will, unfriendliness, (2) wrong
115 by putting in the stocks

130   There shall he sit till noon.

    Regan   Till noon? Till night, my lord, and all night too.

    Kent   Why madam, if I were your father's dog

    You should not use me so.

    Regan   Sir, being[116] his knave, I will.

135   *Cornwall* This is a fellow of the self-same color[117]

    Our sister speaks of. Come, bring away[118] the stocks!

STOCKS ARE BROUGHT OUT

    Gloucester Let me beseech your Grace not to do so.

    His fault is much,[119] and the good King his master

    Will check him for 't. Your purposed low correction[120]

140   Is such as basest and contemnedst[121] wretches

    For pilferings and most common trespasses[122]

    Are punished with.[123] The King must take it ill

    That he's so slightly valued in his messenger

    Should[124] have him thus restrained.

    Cornwall   I'll answer that.

145   *Regan*   My sister may receive it much more worse

    To have her gentleman abused, assaulted

    For following her affairs. Put in his legs.

KENT IS PUT IN THE STOCKS

116 you being
117 sort, nature, character
118 out
119 great
120 purposed low correction = intended abject/base punishment
121 the most despised/scorned/disdained★
122 crimes
123 "His fault . . . punished with": from Quarto
124 that his messenger should be

(*to Cornwall*) Come, my good lord, away.[125]

EXEUNT ALL BUT GLOUCESTER AND KENT

Gloucester I am sorry for thee, friend. 'Tis the Duke's pleasure,
Whose disposition all the world well knows   150
Will not be rubbed[126] nor stopped. I'll entreat for thee.
Kent   Pray do not, sir. I have watched and traveled[127] hard.
Some time[128] I shall sleep out,[129] the rest I'll whistle.
A good man's fortune may grow out at heels.[130]
Give[131] you good morrow.[132]   155
Gloucester The Duke's to blame[133] in this. 'Twill be ill taken.

EXIT GLOUCESTER

Kent   Good King, that must approve[134] the common
saw,[135]
Thou out of heaven's benediction[136] comest[137]
To the warm[138] sun.

125 "For following . . . Come, my good lord, away": from Quarto
126 restrained, influenced, changed
127 (1) journeyed, (2) labored
128 some time = some of the time
129 away
130 out at heels = unfortunate, distressing (as shoes / stockings wear out at the
    heels)
131 I wish
132 morning
133 to blame = at fault
134 demonstrate, prove
135 saying, proverb
136 prosperity, blessing
137 thou out of heaven's benediction comest = you, Lear, descend from the
    comfortable shade of prosperity to something much less comfortable (i.e.,
    people's lives veer from one extreme, either to a worse one or to the
    opposite one)
138 heat of the

160   (*to the just dawning sun*) Approach, thou beacon[139] to this
under[140] globe,
(*taking out a letter*) That by thy comfortable[141] beams I may
Peruse this letter. Nothing almost[142] sees miracles
But misery. I know 'tis from Cordelia,
Who hath most fortunately been informed

165   Of my obscurèd course (*reads aloud*) "and shall[143] find time,
From[144] this enormous state,[145] seeking to give
Losses their remedies."[146] All weary and o'erwatched,[147]
Take vantage,[148] heavy eyes, not to behold
This shameful lodging.[149]

170   Fortune, good night. Smile once more,[150] turn thy wheel![151]

HE SLEEPS

139 watchtower
140 lower
141 strengthening, cheering (COMforTAble)
142 nothing almost = virtually no state of being
143 she will/must
144 being away from/out of
145 enormous state = extraordinary/monstrous/shocking state of things (in Britain)
146 to trying to find ways to supply remedies for what has been lost
147 being awake and observant for too long
148 opportunity ("advantage")
149 accommodation, resting place
150 once more = again
151 as a goddess, Fortune decides who gets good luck, and who gets bad, by spinning a wheel

SCENE 3

A wood

ENTER EDGAR

Edgar I heard myself proclaimed,
  And by the happy[1] hollow of a tree
  Escaped the hunt. No port is free,[2] no place
  That guard[3] and most unusual vigilance
  Does not attend[4] my taking. Whiles[5] I may 'scape,   5
  I will preserve[6] myself, and am bethought[7]
  To take the basest and most poorest shape[8]
  That ever penury,[9] in contempt of[10] man,
  Brought near[11] to beast. My face I'll grime[12] with filth,
  Blanket[13] my loins, elf[14] all my hair in knots,   10
  And with presented nakedness[15] outface[16]
  The winds and persecutions[17] of the sky.

1 lucky, fortunate★
2 unrestricted
3 (noun) watch
4 (1) look/watch for, (2) wait for
5 while, for as long as
6 save
7 disposed, minded
8 appearance
9 destitution, poverty
10 contempt of = dishonoring, despising
11 close, almost
12 smear, blacken
13 (verb) cover, tie around with nothing more than a blanket
14 (verb) tangle
15 presented nakedness = visible/open/displayed bareness (not nudity so
  much as sparsity of covering)
16 (1) confront, defy, (2) overcome
17 annoyances, malignities

The country[18] gives me proof and precedent[19]
Of Bedlam[20] beggars who, with roaring voices,
15   Strike[21] in their numbed and mortified[22] bare arms
Pins, wooden pricks,[23] nails, sprigs[24] of rosemary;
And with this horrible object,[25] from low farms,
Poor pelting[26] villages, sheepcotes,[27] and mills,[28]
Sometime with lunatic bans,[29] sometime with prayers,
20   Enforce their charity.[30] "Poor Turlygod,[31] poor Tom!"[32]
That's something yet.[33] Edgar I nothing am.[34]

EXIT

18 countryside, land, region
19 example, models
20 London asylum for the mentally deranged
21 drive, stick
22 numbed and mortified = unfeeling, insensible, deadened (the two adjectives
    have virtually identical meaning)
23 thorns, spines, prickles, skewers, etc.
24 twigs
25 display
26 petty, insignificant
27 sheds
28 grain-grinding mills
29 proclamations, commands, curses
30 enforce their charity = force/compel the people in these poor conditions
    to give charity
31 (?)
32 often "Tom o' Bedlam" (someone who has previously been incarcerated in
    Bedlam)
33 anyway, still
34 nothing am = am not at all

SCENE 4

In front of Gloucester's castle, Kent in the stocks

ENTER LEAR, FOOL, AND ATTENDANT

Lear   'Tis strange that they should so depart from home,[1]
And not send back my messenger.

Attendant   As I learned,
The night before there was no purpose in them
Of this remove.[2]

Kent   Hail to thee, noble master!

Lear   Ha!   5
Make't thou this shame thy pastime?[3]

Kent   No, my lord.

Fool   Ha, ha! He wears cruel[4] garters. Horses are tied by the
heads, dogs and bears by the neck, monkeys by the loins, and
men by the legs. When a man's over-lusty at[5] legs, then he
wears wooden nether-stocks.[6]   10

Lear   What's he that hath so much thy place mistook
To[7] set thee here?

Kent   It is both he and she,
Your son and daughter.

Lear   No.

Kent   Yes.   15

---

1 their home
2 departure
3 amusement, recreation
4 (1) painful, merciless, (2) crewel worsted (worn by servants)
5 over-lusty at = too lively-legged (i.e., has too many reasons for running away, whether from police or from jealous husbands)
6 nether-stocks = stockings on the lower parts of the legs
7 as to

Lear No, I say.

Kent I say yea.

Lear No, no, they would not.

Kent Yes, they have.

20 *Lear* By Jupiter, I swear no.

Kent By Juno,[8] I swear ay.

Lear   They durst not do 't,

They could not, would not do 't. 'Tis worse than murder,

To do upon respect[9] such violent outrage.

Resolve[10] me, with all modest[11] haste, which way[12]

25 Thou mightst deserve, or they impose, this usage,

Coming[13] from us.

Kent   My lord, when at their home

I did commend[14] your Highness' letters to them,

Ere I was risen from the place[15] that showed

My duty, kneeling, came there a reeking post,[16]

30 Stewed in[17] his haste, half breathless, panting[18] forth

From Goneril his mistress salutations.[19]

Delivered[20] letters, spite of intermission,[21]

8 Jupiter's wife
9 upon respect = rank (the respect due the King)
10 explain to, answer
11 orderly, appropriate, proper
12 how, by what means
13 since you were coming
14 deliver
15 position
16 reeking post = steaming/smoking ("perspiring") rapid messenger★
17 stewed in = boiled by
18 gasping
19 salutations from Goneril, his mistress
20 he delivered
21 interrupting (Kent, still performing his "duty")

Which presently they read, on[22] whose[23] contents,
They summoned up their meiny,[24] straight took horse,
Commanded me to follow and attend   35
The leisure of their answer, gave[25] me cold looks.
And meeting here the other messenger,
Whose welcome I perceived had poisoned mine
(Being[26] the very fellow that of late
Displayed[27] so saucily against your Highness),   40
Having more man than wit about me, drew.
He raised the house with loud and coward cries.
Your son and daughter found this trespass worth
The shame which here it suffers.

Fool Winter's not gone yet, if the wild geese fly that way.   45
   Fathers that wear rags
    Do make their children blind,[28]
   But fathers that bear bags[29]
    Shall see their children kind.
   Fortune, that arrant[30] whore,   50
   Ne'er turns the key[31] to the poor.
   But for all[32] this thou shalt have as many dolors[33] for[34] thy

22 on the basis of, after reading
23 Quarto (Folio: those)
24 following, retinue, train
25 and gave
26 he being
27 made a show of
28 heedless, uncaring
29 of money ("purses": there was then no money in circulation but coins)
30 notorious
31 opens its door
32 for all = in spite of
33 (1) sorrows, (2) dollars (German or Spanish money)
34 from, on account of

daughters as thou canst tell[35] in a year.

Lear   O, how this mother[36] swells up toward my heart!

55   Hysterica passio,[37] down, thou climbing sorrow,

Thy element's[38] below. Where is this daughter?

Kent   With the Earl, sir, here within.

Lear   (*to Attendant*) Follow
me not,

Stay here.

EXIT LEAR

Attendant Made you no more offense but what you speak of?

60   *Kent*   None.

How chance[39] the King comes with so small a train?

Fool   And[40] thou hadst been set i' the stocks for that
question, thou hadst well deserved it.

Kent   Why, Fool?

65   *Fool*   We'll set thee to school to an ant, to teach thee there's
no laboring i' the winter.[41] All that follow their noses are led
by their eyes but[42] blind men, and there's not a nose among
twenty but can smell him[43] that's stinking.[44] Let go thy
hold[45] when a great wheel runs down a hill, lest it break thy

70   neck with following it. But the great one that goes up the

35 count
36 hysteria (seen as a womb/female disease)
37 hysterica passio = hysteria (Latin)
38 proper place
39 does it happen
40 if
41 "the ant . . . provideth her meat [food] in the summer": Proverbs 6:6, 8
42 except for
43 he who
44 i.e., smelling of decay – like Lear
45 grip

hill, let him draw thee after. When a wise man gives thee
better counsel, give me mine again. I would have none but
knaves follow it, since a fool gives it.

That sir[46] which serves and seeks for gain,
   And follows but for form,[47]   75
Will pack when it begins to rain,
   And leave thee in the storm.
But I will tarry, the fool will stay,
   And let the wise man fly.
The knave turns fool that runs away,   80
   The fool no[48] knave, perdy.[49]

ENTER LEAR WITH GLOUCESTER

Kent   Where learned you this, Fool?
Fool   Not i' the stocks, fool.
Lear   Deny[50] to speak with me? They are sick? They are
weary?
They have traveled all the night? Mere fetches,[51]   85
The images of revolt[52] and flying off.[53]
Fetch me a better answer.
Gloucester   My dear lord,
You know the fiery quality of the Duke,
How unremovable[54] and fixed he is

46 that sir = he who
47 appearance, correct procedure
48 is no
49 by God (corruption of "par dieu")
50 say no ("refuse")
51 stratagems, dodges
52 casting off obedience ("rebellion")
53 running away, fleeing
54 immovable

90   In his own course.

      Lear   Vengeance! plague! death! confusion![55]

      Fiery? What quality? Why, Gloucester, Gloucester,

      I'ld[56] speak with the Duke of Cornwall and his wife.

      Gloucester Well my good lord, I have informed them so.

95   *Lear*   Informed them! Dost thou understand me, man?

      Gloucester Ay, my good lord.

      Lear   The King would speak with Cornwall, the dear father

      Would with his daughter speak, commands, tends,[57] service.

      Are they informed of this? My breath and blood!

100   Fiery? The fiery Duke? Tell the hot Duke that –

      No, but not yet, maybe he is not well,

      Infirmity[58] doth still[59] neglect all office

      Whereto[60] our health is bound.[61] We are not ourselves

      When nature, being oppressed, commands the mind

105   To suffer with the body: I'll forbear,

      And am fallen out with my more headier will[62]

      To take[63] the indisposed and sickly[64] fit

      For the sound man. (*notices Kent*) Death on my state!

      Wherefore

      Should he sit here? This act persuades me

110   That this remotion[65] of the Duke and her

55 ruin, destruction
56 I wish to
57 expects
58 sickness
59 always
60 to which
61 tied, fastened, connected
62 more headier will = more headstrong/impetuous desire
63 to take = which takes
64 only sickly
65 remoteness

Is practice only. Give me[66] my servant forth.[67]
(*to Gloucester*) Go tell the Duke, and's wife, I'ld speak with
them.
Now, presently. Bid them come forth and hear me,
Or at their chamber door I'll beat the drum
Till it cry[68] sleep to death.   115
Gloucester I would have all well betwixt you.

EXIT GLOUCESTER

Lear   O me, my heart! My rising heart! But down!
Fool   Cry to it, nuncle, as the cockney did to the eels when
she put 'em i' the paste[69] alive. She knapped 'em o' the
coxcombs with a stick, and cried, "Down, wantons,[70] down!" 120
'Twas her brother[71] that, in pure kindness to his horse,
buttered his hay.[72]

ENTER CORNWALL, REGAN, GLOUCESTER, AND SERVANTS

Lear   Good morrow to you both.
Cornwall   Hail to your Grace!

KENT IS SET AT LIBERTY

Regan   I am glad to see your Highness.
Lear   Regan, I think you are. I know what reason   125
I have to think so. If thou shouldst not be glad

---

66 give me = let
67 out
68 cry/bark after (like a pack of houndes "in cry")
69 pastry
70 bad-mannered/rude animals
71 i.e., a cockney (resident in London)
72 his hay = its hay (which horses will not eat, as country people and
   stablemen know)

I would divorce me from thy mother's tomb,
Sepulchring an adultress. (*to Kent*) O are you free?
Some other time for that. Belovèd Regan,
130 Thy sister's naught. O Regan, she hath tied
Sharp-toothed unkindness, like a vulture, here,
(*points to his heart*) I can scarce speak to thee, thou'lt not believe
With how depraved a quality – O Regan!

Regan I pray you, sir, take patience. I have hope
135 You less know how to value her desert[73]
Than she to scant[74] her duty.

Lear   Say? How is that?

Regan I cannot think my sister in the least
Would fail her obligation. If sir, perchance
She have restrained the riots of your followers,
140 'Tis on such ground, and to such wholesome[75] end,
As clears her from all blame.

Lear   My curses on her!

Regan O sir, you are old.
Nature in you stands on the very verge[76]
Of her confine.[77] You should[78] be ruled and led
145 By some discretion, that discerns[79] your state
Better than you yourself. Therefore I pray you
That to our sister you do make return.

73 deserving (deZERT)
74 cut down, abridge
75 beneficial, salutary
76 boundary, limit
77 frontier, border (CONfine)
78 must
79 recognizes, perceives

Say you have wronged her.

Lear   Ask her forgiveness?

Do you but mark how this becomes the house?[80]

"Dear daughter, I confess that I am old.   150

LEAR KNEELS

Age is unnecessary. On my knees I beg

That you'll vouchsafe[81] me raiment, bed, and food."

Regan   Good sir, no more. These are unsightly[82] tricks.

Return you to my sister.

Lear   (rising) Never, Regan.

She hath abated me of half my train,   155

Looked black[83] upon me, strook[84] me with her tongue

Most serpent-like, upon the very heart.

All the stored[85] vengeances of heaven fall

On her ingrateful top![86] Strike her young bones,

You taking[87] airs, with lameness!

Cornwall   Fie sir. Fie!   160

Lear   You nimble[88] lightnings, dart your blinding flames

Into her scornful eyes! Infect[89] her beauty,

You fen-sucked[90] fogs, drawn by the powerful sun,

To fall and blister!

80 becomes the house = is appropriate / fit for our kingly lineage
81 grant, bestow / confer on
82 ugly
83 frowning, angry, threatening
84 struck
85 accumulated
86 ingrateful top = ungrateful head
87 rapacious, blasting, pernicious
88 swift
89 stain, taint, poison, spoil
90 fen-sucked = drawn from marshes

Regan	O the blest gods!

165 So will you wish on me, when the rash mood is on.

Lear   No Regan, thou shalt never have my curse.

Thy tender-hefted[91] nature shall not give

Thee o'er to harshness. Her eyes are fierce, but thine

Do comfort and not burn. 'Tis not in thee

170 To grudge my pleasures, to cut off my train,

To bandy hasty words, to scant my sizes,[92]

And in conclusion to oppose the bolt[93]

Against my coming in. Thou better know'st

The offices of nature, bond of childhood,

175 Effects of courtesy, dues[94] of gratitude.

Thy half o' the kingdom hast thou not forgot,

Wherein I thee endowed.[95]

Regan   Good sir, to the purpose.[96]

TUCKET WITHIN

Lear   Who put my man i' the stocks?

Cornwall   What trumpet's that?

Regan   I know't, my sister's. This approves her letter,

That she would soon be here.

ENTER OSWALD

180   Is your lady come?

Lear   This is a slave, whose easy-borrowed[97] pride

---

91 tender-hefted = tenderly set/settled/established ("framed")
92 fixed standards/quantities
93 oppose the bolt = set the bolt on the door ("lock the door")
94 debts
95 gave, invested, enriched
96 point, subject, issue
97 easy-borrowed = easily assumed/put on (borrow: take for temporary use)

Dwells in the fickle grace of her he follows.

Out varlet, from my sight!

Cornwall   What means your Grace?

Lear   Who stocked my servant? Regan, I have good hope

Thou didst not know on't. Who comes here? O heavens,   185

ENTER GONERIL

(*to the heavens*) If you do love old men, if your sweet sway

Allow obedience, if you yourselves are old,

Make it your cause.[98] Send down, and take my part!

(*to Goneril*) Art not ashamed to look upon this beard?

O Regan, wilt thou take her by the hand?   190

Goneril   Why not by th' hand sir? How have I offended?

All's not offense that indiscretion[99] finds

And dotage terms so.

Lear   O sides,[100] you are too tough!

Will you yet hold? How came my man i' the stocks?

Cornwall I set him there, sir. But his own disorders[101]   195

Deserved much less advancement.[102]

Lear   You? Did you?

Regan   I pray you, father, being weak, seem so.

If till the expiration of your month

You will return and sojourn with my sister,

Dismissing half your train, come then to me.   200

I am now from home, and out of[103] that provision[104]

98 motive / reason for action★
99 imprudence, lack of judgment
100 i.e., sides of the body
101 violations of order, irregularities of behavior
102 promotion, preferment (ironic)
103 out of = (1) away from, (2) deprived of, without
104 preparations, supplies, necessaries

Which shall be needful for your entertainment.

Lear   Return to her? And fifty men dismissed?

No, rather I abjure[105] all roofs, and choose

205   To wage[106] against the enmity[107] o' the air,[108]

To be a comrade with the wolf and owl –

Necessity's sharp pinch.[109] Return with her?

Why the hot-blooded France, that dowerless took

Our youngest born, I could as well be brought

210   To knee[110] his throne, and squire-like[111] pension beg,

To keep base life afoot. Return with her?

Persuade me rather to be slave and sumpter[112]

To this (*indicating Oswald*) detested groom.

Goneril   At your choice, sir.

Lear   I prithee, daughter, do not make me mad.

215   I will not trouble thee, my child. Farewell.

We'll no more meet, no more see one another.

But yet thou art my flesh, my blood, my daughter,

Or rather a disease that's in my flesh,

Which I must needs call mine. Thou art a boil,

220   A plague-sore, an embossèd carbuncle,[113]

In my corrupted blood. But I'll not chide thee,

Let shame come when it will, I do not call it,

I do not bid the thunder-bearer shoot,

105 renounce, forswear, disclaim, reject
106 fight, venture
107 ill-will, hostility
108 open air ("out of doors")
109 pressure, difficulty ("squeeze")
110 go down on his knees to
111 squire-like = like a servant/personal attendant
112 pack horse
113 embossèd carbuncle = bulging/tumid tumor

Nor tell tales of thee to high-judging[114] Jove.
Mend[115] when thou canst, be better at thy leisure,   225
I can be patient, I can stay with Regan,
I and my hundred knights.

Regan   Not altogether so,[116]
I looked not for you yet, nor am provided
For your fit welcome. Give ear sir, to my sister,
For those that mingle[117] reason with your passion   230
Must be content to think you old, and so —
But she knows what she does.

Lear   Is this well[118] spoken?

Regan   I dare avouch[119] it, sir. What, fifty followers?
Is it not well?[120] What should you need of more?
Yea, or so many? Sith that both charge and danger   235
Speak 'gainst so great a number? How in one house[121]
Should many people, under two commands,
Hold amity?[122] 'Tis hard, almost impossible.

Goneril Why might not you, my lord, receive attendance
From those that she calls servants, or from mine?   240

Regan   Why not, my lord? If then they chanced to slack you,
We could control[123] them. If you will[124] come to me

114 high-judging = judging from on high
115 (1) improve, reform, (2) atone
116 altogther so = completely, entirely (with a further implication: not all of
     you)
117 join
118 (1) correctly, justifiably, suitably, (2) generously, kindly, (3) gratefully
119 confirm, prove, guarantee
120 i.e., isn't fifty enough?
121 speak GAINST so GREAT a NUMber HOW in one HOUSE
122 friendly relations
123 (1) regulate, (2) call to account, rebuke
124 (1) wish to, (2) will in the future

    (For now I spy a danger) I entreat you

    To bring but five and twenty. To no more

    Will I give place or notice.[125]

245 *Lear*   I gave you all –

    Regan   And in good[126] time you gave it.

    Lear   Made you my guardians,[127] my depositaries,[128]

    But kept a reservation to be followed

    With such[129] a number. What, must I come to you

250   With five and twenty? Regan, said you so?

    Regan   And speak't again, my lord, no more[130] with me.

    Lear   Those wicked creatures yet do[131] look well-favored[132]

    When[133] others are more wicked. Not being the worst

    Stands in some rank[134] of praise. (*to Goneril*) I'll go with thee,

255   Thy fifty yet doth double[135] five and twenty,

    And thou art twice her love.

    Goneril   Hear me, my lord.

    What need you five and twenty? Ten? Or five?

    To follow[136] in a house where twice so many

    Have a command to tend you?

    Regan   What need one?

260 *Lear*   O reason[137] not the need. Our basest beggars

---

125 place or notice = room/space or recognition
126 right, proper, seasonable
127 protectors, defenders, keepers
128 trustees ("receptacles")
129 with such = by exactly such
130 than that number
131 yet do = still
132 attractive
133 while, whereas
134 degree ("ordering")
135 (verb)
136 follow/attend you
137 discuss, argue★

Are in the poorest thing superfluous.[138]
Allow not nature more than nature needs,
Man's[139] life's is cheap as beast's. Thou art a lady.
If only to go warm were gorgeous,[140]
Why nature needs not what thou gorgeous wear'st,[141]   265
Which scarcely keeps thee warm. But for true need –
You heavens, give me that patience, patience I need.
You see me here (you gods) a poor old man,
As full of grief as age, wretched in both!
If it be you that stir these daughters' hearts   270
Against their father, fool me not so much
To[142] bear it tamely. Touch me with noble anger,
And let not women's weapons, water drops,
Stain my man's cheeks! No, you unnatural hags,
I will have such revenges on you both,   275
That all the world shall – I will do such things –
What they are, yet I know not, but they shall be
The terrors of the earth! You think I'll weep,
No, I'll not weep.

SOUNDS OF A STORM

I have full cause of weeping. But this heart   280
Shall break into a hundred thousand flaws,[143]

138 are in the poorest thing superfluous = possess more than enough of the
    least valuable things
139 and then man's
140 magnificent, sumptuous, dazzling
141 gorgeous wear'st = gorgeously wear (literally, "wear of that which is
    gorgeous")
142 fool me not so much to = make me not so much a fool as to
143 detached pieces

Or ere[144] I'll weep. O Fool, I shall go mad!

EXEUNT LEAR, GLOUCESTER, KENT, AND FOOL

Cornwall   Let us withdraw, 'twill be a storm.

Regan   This house is little.[145] The old man and's people
285   Cannot be well bestowed.[146]

Goneril   'Tis his own blame, hath put himself from rest,[147]
And must needs taste[148] his folly.

Regan   For his particular,[149] I'll receive him gladly,
But not one follower.

Goneril   So am I purposed.
290   Where is my Lord of Gloucester?

Cornwall   Followed the old man forth, he is returned.

ENTER GLOUCESTER

Gloucester   The King is in high rage.

Cornwall   Whither is he going?

Gloucester   He calls to horse, but will I know not whither.

Cornwall   'Tis best to give him way, he leads[150] himself.

295   Goneril   (to Gloucester) My lord, entreat him by no means[151] to
stay.

Gloucester   Alack,[152] the night comes on, and the bleak[153] winds

---

144 or ere = before
145 not huge (i.e., larger than "little" in current usage)
146 placed, located
147 he has driven/turned/removed himself away from repose ("peace and
      quiet")
148 experience, deal with
149 his particular = he himself
150 guides
151 entreat him by no means = by no means entreat him
152 alas★
153 cold

    Do sorely ruffle.[154] For many miles about

    There's scarce a bush.[155]

Regan   O sir, to willful men

    The injuries[156] that they themselves procure[157]

    Must be their schoolmasters. Shut up your doors,   300

    He is attended with a desperate[158] train,

    And what they may incense[159] him to, being apt[160]

    To have his ear abused, wisdom bids[161] fear.

Cornwall   Shut up your doors, my lord, 'tis a wild night.

    My Regan counsels well. Come out o' the storm.   305

EXEUNT

154 sorely ruffle = severely rage/bluster
155 i.e., they've mostly been blown down/away
156 wrongs, suffering, mischief*
157 contrive, cause
158 with a desperate = by a dangerous/reckless/violent
159 inflame, excite, provoke
160 he being prepared/of a disposition/tendency
161 must

Act 3

❦

SCENE I

A heath

ENTER, FROM OPPOSITE SIDES OF THE STAGE,
KENT AND AN ATTENDANT

Kent　　Who's there, besides foul weather?

Attendant　One minded like[1] the weather, most unquietly.[2]

Kent　　I know you. Where's the King?

Attendant　Contending[3] with the fretful[4] elements,

5　　　　Bids the winds blow the earth into the sea,

　　　　Or swell the curlèd waters 'bove the main,[5]

　　　　That things might change, or cease.

Kent　　　　　　　　　　　But who is with him?

Attendant　None but the Fool, who labors to out-jest

　　　　His heart-strook injuries.

---

1 minded like = disposed/inclined, in sympathy with
2 disturbed
3 struggling, fighting
4 ill-tempered, peevish, restless, inflamed
5 mainland

96

Kent   Sir, I do know you,

    And dare upon the warrant[6] of my note   10

    Commend[7] a dear thing to you. There is division

    (Although as yet the face of it be covered

    With mutual cunning) 'twixt Albany and Cornwall,

    Who have – as who have not, that their great stars[8]

    Throned[9] and set high? – servants, who seem no less,[10]   15

    Which[11] are to France the spies and speculations[12]

    Intelligent[13] of[14] our state. What[15] hath been seen,

    Either in snuffs and packings[16] of the Dukes,

    Or the hard rein[17] which both of them have borne[18]

    Against the old kind King, or something deeper,   20

    Whereof perchance these are but furnishings.[19]

Attendant I will talk further with you.

Kent   No, do not.

    For confirmation that I am much more

    Than my out-wall,[20] open this purse, and take

    What it contains. If you shall see Cordelia   25

6 security, assurance, guarantee

7 entrust, deliver

8 i.e, astrological influences / powers

9 (verb, the subject of which is "stars")

10 inferior, lower ranking *or* who indeed appear to be what they are, servants

11 which servants

12 observers

13 (adjective, modifying both "spies" and "speculations") communicating / bearing information

14 about, on

15 that which

16 snuffs and packings = indignations / resentments and plotting / contriving

17 i.e., like someone who rides a horse hard

18 maintained, asserted

19 mere externals ("signs")

20 outward appearance

(As fear not but you shall), show her this ring
And she will tell you who that fellow is
That yet you do not know. Fie on this storm!
I will go seek the King.

Attendant   Give me your hand.
30 Have you no more to say?

Kent   Few words, but to effect more than all yet,
That when we have found the King – in which your pain[21]
That way, I'll this – he that first lights on[22] him
Holla the other.

EXEUNT AT OPPOSITE ENDS OF THE STAGE

21 trouble, toil, effort
22 lights on = meets, discovers

SCENE 2

Another part of the heath

ENTER LEAR AND FOOL

Lear Blow, winds, and crack[1] your cheeks! Rage, blow
 You cataracts,[2] and hurricanoes[3] spout
 Till you have drenched our steeples, drowned the cocks![4]
 You sulphurous and thought-executing[5] fires,
 Vaunt-couriers[6] to oak-cleaving thunderbolts,   5
 Singe my white head! And thou all-shaking thunder,
 Strike[7] flat the thick rotundity[8] o' the world!
 Crack nature's moulds, all germens[9] spill at once
 That make ingrateful man!

Fool O nuncle, court holy-water[10] in a dry house is better than   10
 this rain-water out o' door. Good nuncle, in,[11] ask thy
 daughters' blessing. Here's a night pities[12] neither wise men
 nor fools.

Lear Rumble thy bellyful! Spit fire, spout rain!
 Nor rain, wind, thunder, fire are my daughters: 15
 I tax[13] not you, you elements, with unkindness.

 1 split
 2 floodgates
 3 (1) waterspouts, (2) hurricanes
 4 weathercocks (figures of birds, spindle-mounted to turn with the wind)
 5 carrying out/performing as swift as thought
 6 vaunt-couriers = advance-guards
 7 beat
 8 state of being round/spherical
 9 seeds
 10 court holy-water = gracious but empty promises
 11 go in
 12 that pities
 13 blame, scold

I never gave you kingdom, called you children,
You owe me no subscription.[14] Then let fall
Your horrible pleasure. Here I stand your slave,
20 A poor, infirm, weak, and despised old man.
But yet I call you servile ministers,[15]
That[16] have with two pernicious[17] daughters joined[18]
Your high-engendered battles[19] 'gainst a head
So old and white as this. O ho, 'tis foul!

25 *Fool* He that has a house to put's head in, has a good headpiece.

The codpiece[20] that will house[21]
    Before the head has any,[22]
The head and he shall louse.[23]
    So[24] beggars marry many.[25]

30   The man that makes his toe
    What he his heart should make,[26]
Shall of[27] a corn cry woe,
    And turn his sleep to wake.[28]

For there was never yet fair woman but she made mouths in a glass.

---

14 submission, allegiance
15 servile ministers = slavish servants
16 you who
17 destructive, ruinous, wicked
18 (verb) (1) united, combined, (2) sent into combat
19 high-engendered battles = loftily begotten/conceived/born troops/ battalions
20 penis (literally, a bagged appendage to close-fitting male outer garments)
21 (verb) engage in sex (literally, "lodge")
22 any housing/lodging
23 be infested with lice
24 thus
25 beggars marry many = many beggars (who are lice-infested) marry
26 i.e., inverts proper values
27 because
28 waking

Lear No, I will be the pattern[29] of all patience,   35
    I will say nothing.

ENTER KENT

Kent Who's there?

Fool Marry, here's grace and a codpiece: that's a wise man and a
    fool.

Kent (to Lear) Alas sir, are you here? Things that love night
    Love not such nights as these. The wrathful skies   40
    Gallow[30] the very wanderers of the dark,[31]
    And make them keep their caves. Since I was[32] man,
    Such sheets of fire, such bursts of horrid thunder,
    Such groans of roaring wind, and rain, I never
    Remember to have heard. Man's nature cannot carry   45
    Th' affliction,[33] nor the fear.

Lear   Let the great gods,
    That keep this dreadful pudder[34] o'er our heads,
    Find out[35] their enemies now. Tremble thou wretch,
    That hast within thee undivulgèd crimes,
    Unwhipped of[36] justice. Hide thee, thou bloody hand –   50
    Thou perjured – and thou simular[37] man of virtue
    That art incestuous. Caitiff,[38] to pieces shake,
    That under covert and convenient seeming

29 model
30 gallow = gally = frighten, daze
31 of the dark = in the darkness
32 have been a
33 misery, distress
34 pudder = pother = turmoil, uproar
35 find out = discover
36 by
37 simulating, pretending
38 villain, wretch

Hast practiced on man's life. Close pent-up guilts,

55 Rive[39] your concealing continents,[40] and cry

These dreadful summoners grace.[41] I am a man

More sinned against than sinning.

Kent   Alack, bareheaded!

Gracious my lord, hard by here is a hovel,[42]

Some friendship[43] will it lend you 'gainst the tempest.

60 Repose you there, while I to this hard[44] house

(More harder than the stones whereof 'tis raised,[45]

Which[46] even but now, demanding after[47] you,

Denied me to come in) return, and force[48]

Their scanted courtesy.[49]

Lear   My wits begin to turn.

65 (to Fool) Come on, my boy. How dost, my boy? Art cold?

I am cold myself. (to Kent) Where is this straw, my fellow?

The art of our necessities is strange,

That can make vile things precious. Come, your[50] hovel.

Poor fool, and knave, I have one part in my heart

70 That's sorry yet for thee.

39 tear apart, split, destroy
40 contents
41 cry these dreadful summoners grace = cry/beg for grace from these terrible bailiffs/arresting officers
42 shed, shack
43 kindliness, favor
44 hard-hearted, impenetrable (the castle, belonging to Gloucester but controlled, now, by Cornwall et al.)
45 built
46 those in the castle
47 demanding after = asking about
48 constrain, press hard upon
49 considerateness
50 we'll go to your

Fool (*sings*)

> He that has and a little tiny wit,
>> With heigh-ho, the wind and the rain,
> Must make content with his fortunes fit,[51]
>> For the rain it raineth every day.   75

Lear True, my good boy. (*to Kent*) Come, bring us to this hovel.

EXEUNT LEAR AND KENT

Fool   This is a brave[52] night to cool a courtesan.[53] I'll speak a
prophecy ere I go:

> When priests are more[54] in word than matter,
> When brewers mar their malt with water,
> When nobles are their tailors' tutors,   80
> No heretics burned, but wenches'[55] suitors,
> When every case in law is right,
> No squire in debt, nor no poor knight,
> When slanders do not live in tongues,
> Nor cutpurses[56] come not to throngs,[57]   85
> When usurers tell their gold i' the field,
> And bawds and whores do churches build,
> Then shall the realm of Albion[58]
> Come to great confusion.[59]

---

51 content with his fortunes fit = make his happiness fit with his luck
52 fine, grand★
53 courtier
54 greater
55 but wenches' = but only girls'/young women's
56 pickpockets
57 (nor CUT purSEZ come NOT to THRONGS)
58 England (ALbeeAWN)
59 ruin, destruction (conFYOOzeeAWN)

90 Then comes the time, who lives[60] to see't,

That going shall be used with feet.[61]

This prophecy Merlin shall make, for I live before his time.

EXIT

---

60 who lives = whoever may live
61 used with feet = done by foot

SCENE 3

Gloucester's castle

Gloucester Alack, alack, Edmund, I like not this unnatural dealing.[1] When I desired their leave that I might pity him, they took from me the use of mine own house, charged me on pain of their perpetual displeasure, neither to speak of him, entreat for him, nor any way sustain him.   5

Edmund   Most savage and unnatural!

Gloucester Go to,[2] say you nothing. There is division betwixt the Dukes, and a worse matter than that. I have received a letter this night, 'tis dangerous to be spoken. I have locked the letter in my closet. These injuries the King now bears will be   10
revenged home,[3] there's part of a power[4] already footed.[5] We must incline to[6] the King. I will look[7] him and privily relieve him. Go you and maintain talk with the Duke, that my charity be not of him perceived. If he ask for me, I am ill, and gone to bed. Though I die for it (as no less is threatened me)   15
the King my old master must be relieved.[8] There is some strange thing toward, Edmund. Pray you, be careful.

1 conduct
2 go to = come, come
3 (1) successfully, (2) thoroughly★
4 army
5 established
6 incline to = take the side of
7 (1) go and see, examine, (2) search for, seek out
8 rescued, helped

Edmund This courtesy forbid thee,[9] shall the Duke
　　Instantly know, and of that letter too.
20　　This seems a fair deserving, and must draw[10] me
　　That which my father loses: no less than all.
　　The younger rises when the old doth fall.

EXIT

9 courtesy forbid thee = considerateness/generosity, which has been
　forbidden to you
10 bring

SCENE 4

The heath, in front of a hovel

ENTER LEAR, KENT, AND FOOL

Kent Here is the place, my lord, good my lord, enter.

The tyranny[1] of the open[2] night's too rough

For nature to endure.

Lear   Let me alone.

Kent Good my lord, enter here.

Lear   Wilt[3] break my heart?

Kent I had rather break mine own. Good my lord, enter.   5

Lear Thou think'st 'tis much that this contentious[4] storm

Invades[5] us to the skin. So 'tis to thee.

But where the greater malady is fixed,[6]

The lesser is scarce felt. Thou'dst shun a bear,

But if thy flight lay toward the raging sea,   10

Thou'dst meet the bear i' the mouth. When the mind's free,

The body's delicate.[7] The tempest in my mind

Doth from my senses take all feeling else,

Save what beats there. Filial ingratitude!

Is it not as[8] this mouth should tear[9] this hand   15

For lifting food to't? But I will punish home.

No, I will weep no more. In such a night

1 oppression, severity, harshness
2 unprotected against, uncovered (i.e., unroofed against)
3 will it
4 quarrelsome
5 penetrates
6 constant, firmly rooted
7 fastidious, dainty, not tough/robust
8 as if
9 lacerate, wound

To shut me out? Pour on, I will endure.
In such a night as this? O Regan, Goneril,
20   Your old kind father, whose frank[10] heart gave all –
O that way madness lies, let me shun that.
No more of that.

Kent   Good my lord, enter here.

Lear Prithee, go in thyself, seek thine own ease.
This tempest will not give me leave to ponder
25   On things would[11] hurt me more. But I'll go in.
(*to Fool*) In, boy; go first. You houseless poverty –
Nay, get thee in. I'll pray, and then I'll sleep.

THE FOOL GOES IN

Poor naked wretches, whereso'er you are,
That bide[12] the pelting[13] of this pitiless storm,
30   How shall your houseless heads, and unfed sides,
Your looped and windowed[14] raggedness, defend you
From seasons such as these? O I have ta'en
Too little care of this! Take physic, pomp,[15]
Expose thyself to feel what wretches feel,
35   · That thou mayst shake the superflux[16] to them,
And show the heavens more just.

---

10 generous, lavish, sincere
11 which would
12 remain/stay in
13 beating down
14 looped and windowed = having holes and openings
15 take physic, pomp = you men of magnificence (pomp), cure yourself by taking a cathartic/purge (i.e., in Lear's following words, "expose yourself . . .")
16 super-/overabundance (i.e., which you possess but do not in fact need)

Edgar (*within*) Fathom and half, fathom and half![17] Poor Tom!

THE FOOL RUNS OUT FROM THE HOVEL

Fool Come not in here nuncle, here's a spirit,[18]
Help me, help me!

Kent   Give me thy hand. Who's there?

Fool A spirit, a spirit, he says his name's poor Tom.   40

Kent What art thou that dost grumble[19] there i' the straw?
Come forth.

ENTER EDGAR DISGUISED AS A MADMAN

Edgar Away, the foul fiend follows me! Through the sharp
hawthorn[20] blows the cold wind. Hum, go to thy cold bed,
and warm thee.   45

Lear Didst thou given all to thy two daughters? And art thou
come to this?

Edgar Who gives any thing to poor Tom? Whom the foul fiend
hath led through fire, and through flame, through ford and
whirlpool, o'er bog and quagmire, that hath laid knives under   50
his pillow, and halters[21] in his pew,[22] set ratsbane[23] by his
porridge, made him proud of heart, to ride on a bay[24]
trotting-horse over four-inched bridges,[25] to course[26] his

---

17 i.e., the depth-measurements ("soundings") taken by sailors
18 ghost, supernatural creature
19 mutter, mumble
20 thorny shrub
21 hanging rope nooses (i.e., the second of a series of three temptations to
suicide)
22 allotted place (usually in church)
23 arsenic ("rat poison")
24 reddish brown
25 four-inched bridges = bridges only four inches wide
26 hunt, pursue

own shadow for a traitor. Bless thy five wits![27] Tom's a-cold.

55 O do, de, do de, do, de. Bless[28] thee from whirlwinds, star-
blasting,[29] and taking,[30] do poor Tom some charity, whom
the foul fiend vexes. There could I have him now (*pounces*),
and there, and there again, and there.

Lear What, have his daughters brought him to this pass?

60 Couldst thou save nothing? Didst thou give them all?

Fool Nay, he reserved a blanket, else we had been all shamed.[31]

Lear Now all[32] the plagues that in the pendulous[33] air
Hang fated o'er men's faults light on thy daughters!

Kent He hath no daughters, sir.

65 *Lear* Death, traitor! Nothing could have subdued nature
To such a lowness but his unkind daughters.
Is it the fashion, that discarded fathers
Should have thus little mercy on[34] their flesh?
Judicious punishment, 'twas this flesh begot

70 Those pelican[35] daughters.

Edgar Pillicock[36] sat on Pillicock-hill,
Alow, alow, loo, loo!

Fool This cold night will turn us all to fools and madmen.

Edgar Take heed o' the foul fiend, obey thy parents, keep thy

27 mental capacities/faculties
28 protect, guard
29 evil influence of malignant stars
30 seizures, attacks of disease
31 i.e., by being obliged to see him naked
32 may all
33 suspended overhead, overhanging
34 shown toward
35 pelicans were believed to feed their blood to their young
36 penis

word justly,[37] swear not, commit[38] not with man's sworn   75
spouse, set not[39] thy sweet-heart on proud array.[40] Tom's a-
cold.

Lear   What hast thou been?

Edgar   A servingman, proud in heart and mind, that curled my
hair, wore gloves[41] in my cap, served the lust of my mistress'   80
heart, and did the act of darkness with her. Swore as many
oaths as I spake words, and broke them in[42] the sweet face of
heaven. One that slept in the contriving of lust, and waked to
do it. Wine loved I deeply, dice dearly, and in woman out-
paramoured[43] the Turk. False of heart, light of ear,[44] bloody   85
of hand, hog in sloth, fox in stealth, wolf in greediness, dog in
madness, lion in prey.[45] Let not the creaking of shoes nor the
rustling of silks betray thy poor heart to woman. Keep thy
foot out of brothels, thy hand out of plackets,[46] thy pen from
lenders' books, and defy the foul fiend. Still through the   90
hawthorn blows the cold wind. Says suum, mun, hey nonny.
Dolphin[47] my boy, my boy, sessa![48] Let[49] him trot by.

Lear   Thou wert better in thy grave than to answer with thy

37 rightfully, uprightly
38 commit adultery
39 set not = don't fix her mind
40 proud array = splendid/magnificent/luxurious clothing
41 i.e., an intimate garment given him by the lady
42 in front of
43 outdid in sexual love
44 light of ear = (?) unthinking (indifferent)? unreliable? credulous?
45 preying
46 slits in the waistline of petticoats
47 a horse?
48 (?) stop? (from French "cessez," stop)
49 (?) well, let

uncovered body this extremity[50] of the skies. Is man no more
95   than this? Consider him well. Thou owest the worm no silk,
the beast no hide, the sheep no wool, the cat[51] no perfume.
Ha? Here's three on's[52] are sophisticated![53] (*to Edgar*) Thou[54]
art the thing itself. Unaccommodated[55] man is no more but[56]
such a poor, bare, forked[57] animal as thou art. Off, off, you
100   lendings![58] Come, unbutton here.[59]

TEARING OFF HIS CLOTHES

Fool   Prithee nuncle, be contented, 'tis a naughty[60] night to
swim in. Now a little fire in a wild[61] field were like an old
lecher's heart – a small spark, all the rest on's[62] body cold.
Look, here comes a walking fire.

ENTER GLOUCESTER, WITH A TORCH

105 *Edgar* This is the foul fiend Flibbertigibbet.[63] He begins at
curfew,[64] and walks till the first cock.[65] He gives the web and

50 extreme state
51 civet
52 of us (i.e., we three here)
53 altered from / deprived of simple naturalness
54 But you
55 unprovided-for
56 no more but = nothing more than
57 i.e., divided ("forked") at the latter end of the trunk by a pair of legs
58 loans, borrowings (i.e., clothes)
59 his own clothes
60 wicked, bad★
61 uncultivated, gone to brush
62 of his
63 (1) name of a devil, (2) a frivolous / flighty woman
64 9:00 P.M.
65 just before dawn

the pin,[66] squints[67] the eye, and makes the harelip, mildews
the white[68] wheat, and hurts the poor creature[69] of earth.
    Swithold[70] footed[71] thrice the 'old,[72]
    He met the night-mare,[73] and her nine-fold,[74]   110
        Bid her alight,[75]
        And her troth plight,[76]
    And aroint[77] thee witch, aroint thee!

Kent   (to Lear) How fares your Grace?

Lear   (indicating Edgar) What's he?   115

Kent   (to Edgar) Who's there? What is't you seek?

Gloucester What are you there? Your names?

Edgar   Poor Tom, that eats the swimming frog, the toad, the
           tadpole, the wall-newt[78] and the water.[79] That in the fury[80]
           of his heart, when the foul fiend rages, eats cow-dung for   120
           sallets,[81] swallows the old rat and the ditch-dog,[82] drinks the

---

66 the web and the pin = an eye disease, the eye being covered by a film, and
   there being an excrescence the size of a pinhead ("cataract")
67 (verb) causes the eye to squint/be crossed
68 ripening
69 (plural) creatures that live on this earth
70 Saint Withold, patron saint of nocturnal travelers
71 walked
72 wold = open country
73 female nighttime spirit that attacks sleeping people, lying on them and
   afflicting them with her weight
74 nine attending creatures ("familiars")
75 i.e., get off the people she is attacking
76 troth plight = promise/pledge her agreement to desist
77 go away, begone ("avaunt"*)
78 newt (amphibian lizard) on the wall
79 the newt in the water
80 disorder, tumult
81 salads
82 dead dog in a ditch

green mantle[83] of the standing pool. Who is whipped from
tithing to tithing,[84] and stock- punished, and imprisoned.
Who hath had three suits to his back, six shirts to his body,[85]
125   Horse to ride, and weapon to wear,

  But mice and rats, and such small deer,

  Have been Tom's food for seven long year.

Beware my follower.[86] Peace, Smulkin,[87] peace, thou fiend!

Gloucester What, hath your Grace no better company?

130 *Edgar*   The prince of darkness[88] is a gentleman.

  Modo he's call'd, and Mahu.[89]

Gloucester Our flesh and blood is grown so vile, my lord,

  That it doth hate what gets[90] it.

Edgar   Poor Tom's a-cold.

135 *Gloucester* Go in with me. My duty cannot suffer

  T' obey in all your daughters' hard commands.

  Though their injunction be to bar my doors,

  And let this tyrannous night take hold upon you,

  Yet have I ventured to come seek you out,

140   And bring you where both fire and food is ready.

Lear   First let me talk with this philosopher.[91]

  What is the cause of thunder?

Kent   Good my lord, take his offer, go into the house.

---

83 scum
84 tithing to tithing = one parish to another
85 as a servant, which Edgar claims to have been
86 (1) servant, (2) familiar
87 a minor devil
88 Satan
89 Modu . . . Mahu = minor devils
90 (?) profits? begets, procreates, spawns?
91 Edgar

Lear	I'll talk a word with this same learned Theban.[92]

What is your study?   145

Edgar	How to prevent[93] the fiend, and to kill vermin.
Lear	Let me ask you one word in private.
Kent	(*to Gloucester*) Importune him once more to go, my

lord.

His wits begin to unsettle.

Gloucester   Canst thou blame him?

His daughters seek his death. Ah, that good Kent,   150
He said it would be thus. Poor banished man.
Thou sayest the King grows mad. I'll tell thee, friend,
I am almost mad myself. I had a son,
Now outlawed from my blood. He sought my life
But[94] lately, very late. I loved him (friend),   155
No father his son dearer. True to tell thee,
The grief hath crazed my wits. What a night's this!
(*to Lear*) I do beseech your Grace –

Lear   O cry you mercy,[95] sir.

Noble philosopher, your company.[96]

Edgar	Tom's a-cold. 160
Gloucester	In, fellow, there, into th' hovel, keep thee warm.
Lear	Come, let's in all.
Kent	This way, my lord.
Lear	With him,

I will keep still[97] with my philosopher.

92 Greek philosopher
93 prepare for, forestall, balk, stop
94 just
95 cry you mercy = I beg your pardon
96 society, fellowship
97 always

Kent	Good my lord, soothe[98] him, let him take the fellow.
165 *Gloucester*	(*to Kent*) Take him you on.[99]
Kent	Sirrah, come on, go along with us.
Lear	Come, good Athenian.
Gloucester	No words, no words. Hush.
Edgar	Child[100] Rowland to the dark tower came,

170   His word was still,[101] "Fie, foh, and fum,

     I smell the blood of a British man."

EXEUNT

98 humor
99 take him you on = you bring him in
100 title for a candidate to knighthood
101 his word was still = what he said was always

SCENE 5

Gloucester's castle

ENTER CORNWALL AND EDMUND

Cornwall I will have my revenge ere I depart his[1] house.

Edmund How, my lord, I may be censured (that nature thus
  gives way to loyalty), something fears me to think of.

Cornwall I now perceive, it was not altogether your brother's evil
  disposition made him seek his[2] death, but a provoking merit,[3]   5
  set a-work by a reprovable[4] badness in himself.[5]

Edmund How malicious is my fortune, that I must repent to be
  just? This is the letter he[6] spoke of, which approves him an
  intelligent[7] party to the advantages of France. O heavens!
  That this treason were not, or not I the detector!   10

Cornwall Go with me to the Duchess.

Edmund If the matter of this paper be certain,[8] you have
  mighty business in hand.

Cornwall True or false, it hath made thee Earl of Gloucester.
  Seek out where thy father is, that he may be ready for our   15
  apprehension.[9]

Edmund (*aside*) If I find him comforting the King, it will stuff
  his[10] suspicion more fully. (*to Cornwall*) I will persevere in my

1 Gloucester's
2 Gloucester's
3 provoking merit = exasperated/irritated/angered deserved reward
4 blameworthy, reprehensible
5 Gloucester
6 Gloucester
7 knowing, spying
8 definite, unfailing
9 seizing, capturing
10 stuff his = augment/reinforce Cornwall's

course of loyalty, though the conflict be sore between that
20   and my blood.

Cornwall I will lay trust upon thee. And thou shalt find a dear
father in my love.

EXEUNT

SCENE 6

A room in a farmhouse adjoining the castle

ENTER GLOUCESTER, KING LEAR, KENT,
FOOL, AND EDGAR

Gloucester Here is better than the open air, take it thankfully. I
will piece out[1] the comfort with what addition I can. I will
not be long from[2] you.

Kent All the power of his wits have given way to his
impatience.[3] The gods reward your kindness.   5

EXIT GLOUCESTER

Edgar Frateretto[4] calls me, and tells me Nero[5] is an angler in
the lake of darkness. Pray, innocent, and beware the foul
fiend.

Fool Prithee, nuncle, tell me whether a madman be a
gentleman or a yeoman?[6]   10

Lear A king, a king!

Fool No, he's a yeoman that has a gentleman to his son, for
he's a mad yeoman that sees his son a gentleman before him.

Lear To have a thousand with red burning spits[7]
Come hizzing[8] in upon 'em![9]   15

Edgar Bless thy five wits.

---

1 piece out = enlarge, extend
2 away from
3 restless incapacity
4 a minor devil
5 1ST C. B.C.E. Roman emperor with a bad reputation
6 high-ranking servant
7 pointed metal cooking tools
8 hissing, whizzing
9 Goneril and Regan

Fool　He's mad that trusts in the tameness of a wolf, a horse's
　　health, a boy's love, or a whore's oath.

Lear　It shall be done, I will arraign[10] them straight.[11]

20　*Kent*　O pity! Sir, where is the patience now,
　　That thou so oft have boasted to retain?

Edgar (*aside*)　My tears begin to take his part so much,
　　They'll mar my counterfeiting.

Lear　The little dogs and all,

25　　Tray, Blanch, and Sweetheart, see, they bark at me.

Edgar　Tom will throw[12] his head at them. Avaunt, you curs!
　　　Be thy mouth or black or white,
　　　Tooth that poisons if it bite,
　　　Mastiff, greyhound, mongrel grim,[13]
30　　　Hound or spaniel, brach or him,[14]
　　　Or bobtail tike[15] or trundle-tail,[16]
　　　Tom will make them weep and wail.
　　　For with throwing thus my head,
　　　Dogs leap the hatch, and all are fled.
35　　Do de, de, de. Sessa! Come, march to wakes and fairs and
　　market towns. Poor Tom, thy horn[17] is dry.

Lear　Then let them anatomize[18] Regan, see what breeds about
　　her heart. Is there any cause in nature that makes these hard
　　hearts? (*to Edgar*) You sir, I entertain for one of my hundred,

10 condemn, sentence
11 "He's mad that trusts . . . arraign them straight": Quarto
12 (?) twist, turn, swing (or "throw," since Edgar too is supposed to be mad)
13 fierce, savage
14 brach or him = female or male
15 dog of little worth
16 (?) dragging tail? long-tailed?
17 drinking horn
18 dissect

only I do not like the fashion of your garments. You will say   40
they are Persian, but let them be changed.

Kent   Now good my lord, lie here and rest awhile.

Lear   Make no noise, make no noise, draw the curtains.[19]

So, so, so. We'll go to supper i' the morning.

Fool   And I'll go to bed at noon.   45

ENTER GLOUCESTER

Gloucester Come hither friend. Where is the King my master?

Kent   Here sir, but trouble him not, his wits are gone.

Gloucester Good friend, I prithee, take him in thy arms.

I have o'erheard a plot of death upon him.

There is a litter[20] ready, lay him in 't,   50

And drive toward Dover,[21] friend, where thou shalt meet

Both welcome and protection. Take up thy master.

If thou shouldst dally half an hour, his life,

With thine, and all that offer to defend him,

Stand in assured loss. Take up, take up,   55

And follow me, that will to some provision[22]

Give thee quick conduct.[23] Come, come, away!

EXEUNT

19 bed curtains
20 vehicle, pulled by animals, containing a bed for the sick/wounded
21 seaport in SE England, directly across from France
22 necessaries
23 guidance, direction

SCENE 7

Gloucester's castle

ENTER CORNWALL, REGAN, GONERIL,
EDMUND, AND SERVANTS

Cornwall (*to Goneril*) Post speedily to my lord your husband,
show him this letter, the army of France is landed. (*to Servants*)
Seek out the villain Gloucester.

EXEUNT SOME OF THE SERVANTS

   Regan   Hang him instantly.

5   *Goneril*   Pluck out his eyes.

   Cornwall Leave him to my displeasure. Edmund, keep you our
sister[1] company. The revenges we are bound to take upon
your traitorous father are not fit for your beholding. Advise
the Duke,[2] where you are going, to a most festinate[3]

10   preparation.[4] We are bound to the like. Our posts shall be
swift and intelligent betwixt us. Farewell, dear sister. (*to
Edmund*) Farewell, my Lord of Gloucester.

ENTER OSWALD

    How now? Where's the King?

   Oswald   My Lord of Gloucester hath conveyed him hence.

15   Some five or six and thirty of his knights,
Hot questrists[5] after him, met him at[6] gate,

---

1 Goneril
2 Albany
3 hasty, hurried
4 i.e., military
5 searchers, seekers
6 at the

Who, with some other of the lord's[7] dependants,
Are gone with him toward Dover, where they boast
To have well-armed friends.

Cornwall   Get horses for your mistress.

Goneril   Farewell sweet[8] lord, and sister.   20

Cornwall   Edmund, farewell.

EXEUNT GONERIL, EDMUND, AND OSWALD

                    Go seek the traitor Gloucester,
Pinion[9] him like a thief, bring him before us.

EXEUNT OTHER SERVANTS

Though well we may not pass upon his life[10]
Without the form[11] of justice, yet our power
Shall do a courtesy to our wrath, which men   25
May blame, but not control. Who's there? The traitor?

ENTER GLOUCESTER, BROUGHT IN BY TWO OR THREE

Regan   Ingrateful fox![12] 'Tis he.

Cornwall   Bind fast[13] his corky[14] arms.

Gloucester What mean[15] your Graces? Good my friends,
    consider,
    You are my guests. Do me no foul play, friends.

7 Gloucester's
8 agreeable
9 shackle, tie
10 pass upon his life = sentence him to death
11 proper legal procedure
12 i.e., artful/cunning creature
13 tightly, thoroughly
14 withered, dry
15 have in mind, intend★

Cornwall Bind him, I say.

SERVANTS BIND HIM

30 *Regan*   Hard,[16] hard. O filthy traitor!

Gloucester Unmerciful lady as you are, I'm none.[17]

Cornwall To this chair bind him. Villain, thou shalt find –

REGAN PLUCKS[18] HIS BEARD

Gloucester By the kind gods, 'tis most ignobly[19] done

To pluck me by the beard.

Regan   So white, and such a traitor!

35 *Gloucester*   Naughty lady,

These hairs which thou dost ravish[20] from my chin

Will quicken[21] and accuse thee. I am your host.

With robbers' hands my hospitable favors[22]

You should not ruffle[23] thus. What will you do?

40 *Cornwall* Come sir, what letters had you late from France?

Regan Be simple[24]-answered, for we know the truth.

Cornwall And what confederacy[25] have you with the traitors

Late footed[26] in the kingdom?

Regan   To whose hands have you sent the lunatic King?

Speak.

16 exceedingly, very tightly
17 no traitor
18 pulls hair out of (as one plucks feathers from chickens)
19 basely, dishonorably, meanly
20 take by violence
21 come to life
22 hospitable favors = welcoming face/features (HOSpiTAble)
23 handle roughly
24 simple = straightforward/honest
25 alliance
26 set ("landed")

Gloucester I have a letter guessingly[27] set down,   45
   Which came from one that's of a neutral heart,
   And not from one opposed.

Cornwall   Cunning.

Regan   And false.

Cornwall Where hast thou sent the King?

Gloucester   To Dover.

Regan   Wherefore to Dover? Wast thou not charged[28] at
   peril –

Cornwall Wherefore to Dover? Let him first answer that.   50

Gloucester   I am tied to the stake, and I must stand the
   course.[29]

Regan   Wherefore to Dover, sir?

Gloucester Because I would not[30] see thy cruel nails
   Pluck out his poor old eyes, nor thy fierce sister
   In his anointed[31] flesh stick boarish[32] fangs.   55
   The sea, with such a storm as his bare head
   In hell-black night endured, would have buoyed[33] up
   And quenched the stellèd[34] fires.
   Yet poor old heart, he holp[35] the heavens to rain.
   If wolves had at thy gate howled that stern[36] time,   60

27 conjecturally
28 commanded
29 stand the course = endure being tortured like a bear tied to a stake and set
   on by dogs
30 would not = did not wish to
31 consecrated (as kings were considered to be)
32 cruel (like the fangs of a wild boar)
33 swelled
34 stellar ("studded with stars")
35 helped
36 hard, grim

Thou shouldst[37] have said, "Good porter, turn the key."[38]
All cruels else subscribe.[39] But I shall see
The wingèd vengeance[40] overtake such children.
Cornwall   See't shalt thou never. Fellows, hold the chair.
65   Upon these eyes of thine I'll set my foot.[41]
Gloucester   He that will think to live till he be old,
        Give me some help!

CORNWALL PUTS OUT ONE OF GLOUCESTER'S EYES

                    O cruel! O you gods!
Regan   One side will mock[42] another. Th' other too.
Cornwall   If you see vengeance –
Servant 1   Hold your hand, my lord.
70   I have served you ever since I was a child.
        But better service have I never done you
        Than now to bid you hold.
Regan   How now, you dog!
Servant 1 (*to Regan*) If you did wear a beard upon your chin,
        I'd shake it on this quarrel. What do you mean?
75   *Cornwall*   My villain?

THEY DRAW AND FIGHT

Servant 1 Nay then come on,[43] and take the chance of anger.

CORNWALL IS WOUNDED

37 would
38 i.e., lock the door
39 all cruels else subscribe = all other varieties of cruelty agree with you
40 i.e., wingèd because descending from the heavens, sent by the gods
41 set my foot = suppress, put down, subdue, quell
42 ridicule
43 advance, attack (i.e., a challenge)

Regan   (*to Servant 2*) Give me thy sword. A peasant stand[44] up
    thus!

SHE STABS SERVANT I FROM BEHIND

Servant 1 O I am slain! (*to Gloucester*) My lord, you have one eye
    left
    To see some mischief on[45] him. O!

SERVANT I DIES

Cornwall Lest it see more, prevent it. Out, vile jelly!   80
    Where is thy luster[46] now?
Gloucester All dark and comfortless. Where's my son Edmund?
    Edmund, enkindle all the sparks of nature,
    To quit[47] this horrid act.
Regan   Out,[48] treacherous villain,
    Thou call'st on him that hates thee. It was he   85
    That made the overture[49] of thy treasons to us,
    Who[50] is too good to pity thee.
Gloucester O my follies! Then Edgar was abused.
    Kind gods, forgive me that, and prosper him!
Regan   Go thrust him out at[51] gates, and let him smell   90
    His way to Dover.

EXIT SERVANT WITH GLOUCESTER

44 rise
45 done to him
46 shine, light, glow
47 redeem ("revenge")
48 impossible ("out of the question")
49 revelation, disclosure
50 he who
51 at the

How is't, my lord? How look you?[52]

Cornwall I have received a hurt. Follow me, lady.
Turn out that eyeless villain. Throw this slave[53]
95   Upon the dunghill.[54] Regan, I bleed apace,[55]
Untimely[56] comes this hurt. Give me your arm.

EXIT CORNWALL, LED BY REGAN

52 look you = does it look for you ("how are you")
53 Servant 1
54 garbage heap
55 heavily ("quickly")
56 badly timed, unluckily

Act 4

⚜

SCENE I

The heath[1]

ENTER EDGAR

Edgar Yet better thus, and known to be contemned,
  Than still[2] contemned and flattered to be worst.
  The lowest and most dejected thing of fortune
  Stands still in esperance,[3] lives not in fear.
  The lamentable change is from the best,
  The worst returns[4] to laughter. Welcome, then,   5
  Thou unsubstantial[5] air that I embrace!
  The wretch that thou hast blown unto the worst
  Owes nothing to thy blasts.

  ENTER GLOUCESTER, LED BY AN OLD MAN

1 waste/uncultivated land
2 always
3 hope, expectation
4 changes
5 without real substance/existence

But who comes here?

10   My father, poorly led?[6] World, world, O world!
      But[7] that thy strange mutations[8] make us hate thee,
      Life would not yield to age.[9]

Old Man   O, my good lord,
      I have been your tenant, and your father's tenant,
      These fourscore years.

15 *Gloucester* Away, get thee away. Good friend, be gone,
      Thy comforts can do me no good at all,
      Thee, they may hurt.

Old Man   You cannot see your way.

Gloucester I have no way, and therefore want no eyes.
      I stumbled when I saw. Full oft 'tis seen,
20   Our means secure[10] us, and our mere[11] defects
      Prove our commodities.[12] O dear son Edgar,
      The food[13] of thy abusèd[14] father's wrath.
      Might I but live to see thee in[15] my touch
      I'ld say I had eyes again.

Old Man   How now? Who's there?

25 *Edgar*   (*aside*) O gods! Who is't can say "I am at the worst"?
      I am worse than e'er I was.

Old Man   'Tis poor mad Tom.

---

6 poorly led = being in a state of poverty and being led/conducted along
7 except
8 changes, alterations
9 old age
10 means secure = resources/wealth/money makes us careless/overconfident
11 downright/absolute/sheer
12 prove our commodities = prove to be our resources
13 offspring, creature
14 misled, deceived
15 by means of, in

Edgar   (*aside*) And worse I may be yet. The worst is not
   So long as we can say, "This is the worst."

Old Man Fellow, where goest?

Gloucester   Is it a beggar-man?

Old Man Madman and beggar too.   30

Gloucester He has some reason, else he could not beg.
   I' the last night's storm I such a fellow saw,
   Which made me think a man a worm. My son
   Came then into my mind, and yet my mind
   Was then scarce friends[16] with him. I have heard[17]   35
   more since.
   As flies to wanton boys are we to the gods,
   They kill us for their sport.

Edgar   (*aside*) How should this be?
   Bad is the trade[18] that must play fool to sorrow,
   Angering itself and others. (*aloud*) Bless thee, master.

Gloucester Is that the naked fellow?

Old Man   Ay, my lord.   40

Gloucester Get thee away. If for my sake,
   Thou wilt o'ertake us, hence a mile or twain
   I' the[19] way toward Dover, do it for ancient[20] love,
   And bring some covering for this naked soul,
   Who I'll entreat to lead me.

Old Man   Alack, sir, he is mad.   45

Gloucester 'Tis the time's plague, when madmen lead the blind.

16 intimately acquainted
17 learned
18 (1) way of life, (2) craft, employment
19 i' the = along/on the
20 former, past

Do as I bid thee, or rather do thy pleasure.

Above the rest, be gone.

Old Man   I'll bring him the best 'parel that I have,

50   Come on't[21] what will.

Gloucester   Sirrah, naked fellow.

Edgar   Poor Tom's a-cold. (*aside*) I cannot daub[22] it further.

Gloucester   Come hither, fellow.

Edgar   (*aside*) And yet I must. (*aloud*) Bless thy sweet eyes, they bleed.

55   *Gloucester*   Know'st thou the way to Dover?

Edgar   Both stile[23] and gate, horse-way and foot-path. Poor Tom hath been scared out of his good wits. Bless thee, good man's son, from the foul fiend.

Gloucester   Here, take this purse, thou whom the heavens' plagues

60   Have humbled to all strokes. That I am wretched Makes thee the happier. Heavens, deal so still![24] Let[25] the superfluous and lust-dieted man[26] That slaves your ordinance,[27] that will not see Because he doth not feel, feel your power quickly.

65   So distribution[28] should undo excess, And each man have enough. Dost thou know Dover?

---

21 of/because of it

22 cloak, lay it on

23 steps, rungs, etc., to allow passage over a fence

24 always

25 Heavens, let

26 superfluous and lust-dieted man = the man with overabundant resources who lives for pleasure

27 slaves your ordinance = enslaves (by abusing it) your rules/arrangements

28 redistribution, reallotment, dividing up, dealing out

Edgar   Ay, master.

Gloucester There is a cliff, whose high and bending head[29]
    Looks fearfully in[30] the confinèd deep.[31]
    Bring me but to the very brim of it,   70
    And I'll repair[32] the misery thou dost bear
    With something rich about[33] me. From that place
    I shall no leading need.

Edgar   Give me thy arm.
    Poor Tom shall lead thee.

EXEUNT

---

29 bending head = curving/inclined top
30 fearfully in = frighteningly down on
31 confinèd deep = enclosed sea (the Straits of Dover: looks FEARfulLY in
    THE conFINed DEEP)
32 mend
33 that I have on/with me

SCENE 2

In front of Albany's palace

ENTER GONERIL AND EDMUND

Goneril Welcome,[1] my lord. I marvel our mild[2] husband
    Not met us on the way.

ENTER OSWALD

               Now, where's your master'?
Oswald Madam, within, but never man so changed.
    I told him of the army that was landed.
5   He smiled at it. I told him you were coming,
    His answer was, "The worse."[3] Of Gloucester's treachery,
    And of the loyal service of his[4] son,
    When I informed him, then he called me sot,[5]
    And told me I had turned the wrong side out.
10   What most he should dislike seems pleasant to him,
    What like, offensive.
Goneril   (*to Edmund*) Then shall you go no
    further.
    It is the cowish[6] terror of his spirit
    That dares not undertake. He'll not feel wrongs
    Which tie him to an answer. Our wishes on the way
15   May prove effects. Back Edmund to my brother,

1 to my home: she has come with him, but it is her home they have come to
2 gracious, courteous
3 the worse = so much the worse
4 Gloucester's
5 fool, blockhead, dolt
6 cowardly

Hasten his musters,[7] and conduct his powers.
I must change names[8] at home, and give the distaff[9]
Into my husband's hands. This trusty servant[10]
Shall pass between us. Ere long you are like to hear
(If you dare venture in your own behalf)   20
A mistress's[11] command. Wear this, spare[12] speech.
(*puts chain around his neck*) Decline your head. This kiss, if it
durst speak,
Would stretch[13] thy spirits up into the air.
Conceive,[14] and fare thee well.

Edmund   Yours in the ranks of death.

Goneril   My most dear Gloucester.   25

EXIT EDMUND

O, the difference of man and man!
To thee a woman's services[15] are due,
My fool[16] usurps my body.

Oswald   Madam, here comes my lord.

EXIT OSWALD

ENTER ALBANY

7 assembling of soldiers
8 descriptions (i.e., her coward husband is not a man, so she must become one)
9 women's work (distaff: tool used in spinning)
10 Oswald
11 lady love's, sweetheart's
12 refrain from
13 extend, expand, lift
14 consider, think
15 love's services
16 Albany

Goneril   I have been worth the whistle.[17]

30 **Albany**   O Goneril,
You are not worth the dust which the rude wind
Blows in your face.

Goneril   Milk-livered[18] man,
That bear'st a cheek for blows, a head for wrongs,
Who hast not in thy brows an eye discerning
Thine honor from thy suffering.

35 **Albany**   See thyself, devil!
Proper deformity[19] seems not in the fiend
So horrid as in woman.

Goneril   O vain fool!

ENTER A MESSENGER

Messenger O my good lord, the Duke of Cornwall's dead,
Slain by his servant, going[20] to put out
The other eye of Gloucester.

40 **Albany**   Gloucester's eye!

Messenger A servant that he bred, thrilled[21] with remorse,
Opposed[22] against the act, bending[23] his sword
To[24] his great master, who thereat enraged
Flew on[25] him, and amongst[26] them felled him[27] dead,

---

17 i.e., like a dog that is called by a whistle from its master
18 milk-livered = cowardly
19 proper deformity = personal crookedness/moral disfigurement
20 while going
21 pierced, overwhelmed
22 set himself
23 directing, leveling, aiming
24 at
25 flew on = rushed/ran/sprang at
26 between
27 the servant

But not without that harmful stroke, which since   45
Hath plucked him after.[28]

Albany   This shows you are above,[29]
You justicers,[30] that these our nether[31] crimes
So speedily can venge! But (O poor Gloucester)
Lost he his other eye?

Messenger   Both, both, my lord.
This letter, madam, craves a speedy answer.   50
'Tis from your sister.

Goneril   (*aside*) One way I like this well,
But being widow, and my Gloucester with[32] her,
May all the building[33] in my fancy pluck
Upon[34] my hateful life.[35] Another way
The news is not so tart.[36] (*aloud*) I'll read, and answer.   55

EXIT GONERIL

Albany   Where was his son when they did take his eyes?
Messenger Come with[37] my lady hither.
Albany   He is not here.
Messenger No, my good lord, I met[38] him back again.
Albany   Knows he the wickedness?

28 plucked him after = pulled/taken Cornwall too to death
29 i.e., in the heavens
30 administers of justice
31 earthly ("lower")
32 being with
33 constructing ("castles in the air")
34 pluck upon = pull down, demolish
35 hateful life = my hateful existence with a man like Albany
36 grievous, painful, severe (i.e., because Cornwall's death will more readily
   permit a centralization of power)
37 toward, to
38 found, came across

60   *Messenger* Ay, my good lord. 'Twas he informed against him,[39]
        And quit the house on purpose, that[40] their punishment
        Might have the freer course.

  Albany   Gloucester, I live
        To thank thee for the love thou show'dst the King,
        And to revenge thine eyes. Come hither, friend,
65   Tell me what more thou know'st.

EXEUNT

39 Gloucester
40 so that

SCENE 3[1]

The French camp near Dover

ENTER KENT AND AN ATTENDANT

Kent   Why the King of France is so suddenly gone back,[2]
know you no reason?

Attendant Something he left imperfect[3] in the state, which since
his coming forth is thought of, which imports[4] to the
kingdom so much fear and danger that his personal return   5
was most required and necessary.

Kent   Who hath he left behind him general?[5]

Attendant The Marshal of France, Monsieur La Far.

Kent   Did your letters pierce the Queen[6] to any
demonstration of grief?

Attendant Ay sir she took them, read them in my presence,   10
And now and then an ample tear trilled[7] down
Her delicate cheek. It seemed she was a queen
Over her passion, who most rebel-like,
Sought to be king o'er her.

Kent   O, then it moved her.

Attendant Not to a rage. Patience and sorrow strove   15
Who should express her goodliest.[8] You have[9] seen

---

1 Scene 3 in its entirety is from Quarto; Folio omits it; see Introduction
2 to France
3 unfinished, incomplete
4 causes, brings, carries with it★
5 as general / commanding officer
6 Cordelia
7 flowed
8 the best
9 would have

Sunshine and rain at once. Her smiles and tears
Were like a better way, those happy smilets,[10]
That played on her ripe[11] lip, seemed not to know
20   What guests[12] were in her eyes, which parted thence
As pearls from diamonds dropped. In brief,
Sorrow would be a rarity most beloved,
If all could so become[13] it.

Kent   Made she no verbal question?

Attendant 'Faith,[14] once or twice she heaved[15] the name of
    "father"
25   Pantingly forth, as if it pressed her heart,
Cried, "Sisters, sisters, shame of ladies, sisters!
Kent, father, sisters! What, i' the storm? I' the night?
Let pity not be believed!"[16] There she shook
The holy water from her heavenly eyes,
30   And clamor[17] moistened her, then away she started
To deal with grief alone.

Kent   It is the stars,

The stars above us, govern[18] our conditions,[19]
Else one self[20] mate and make[21] could not beget

10 little/slight smiles
11 full red
12 i.e., tears
13 grace, befit
14 in faith, truly
15 sighed
16 believed in, trusted
17 emotional storminess
18 that govern
19 natures
20 unified self
21 mate and make = one of a pair ("partner") and peer/equal ("mate")

Such different issues.[22] You spoke not with her since?

Attendant No.   35

Kent Was this before the King returned?[23]

Attendant   No, since.

Kent Well sir, the poor distressèd Lear's i' the town,
Who sometime in his better tune,[24] remembers
What we are come about, and by no means
Will yield[25] to see his daughter.

Attendant   Why, good sir?   40

Kent A sovereign shame so elbows[26] him, his own
unkindness,[27]
That stripped her from his benediction, turned her
To foreign casualties,[28] gave her dear rights
To his dog-hearted daughters, these things sting
His mind so venomously, that burning shame   45
Detains him from Cordelia.

Attendant   Alack, poor gentleman!

Kent Of Albany's and Cornwall's powers you heard not?

Attendant 'Tis so, they are afoot.

Kent Well sir, I'll bring you to our master Lear,
And leave you to attend him. Some dear cause   50
Will in concealment wrap me up awhile.

22 offspring, children
23 to France
24 frame of mind, disposition, mood
25 agree, assent, submit
26 prods, pushes, forces
27 a SOvrin SHAME so ELbows HIM his OWN unKINDness: a hexameter
   line (such metrical variations are not uncommon in Shakespeare's plays)
28 uncertainties, precariousness

When I am known aright,[29] you shall not grieve,
Lending me this acquaintance.[30] I pray you, go
Along with me.

EXEUNT

29 correctly, truly
30 personal knowledge

SCENE 4

The same, a tent

ENTER, WITH DRUMS AND COLORS,[1] CORDELIA,
DOCTOR, AND SOLDIERS

Cordelia Alack, 'tis he, why, he was met even now
   As mad as the vexed sea, singing aloud,
   Crowned with rank fumitor[2] and furrow-weeds,[3]
   With hor-lochs,[4] hemlock,[5] nettles, cuckoo-flowers,[6]
   Darnel,[7] and all the idle weeds that grow   5
   In our sustaining corn.[8] A century[9] send forth,
   Search every acre in the high-grown field,
   And bring him to our eye.[10]

EXIT OFFICER

                    What can man's[11] wisdom,
   In the restoring his bereavèd[12] sense?
   He that can help him, take all my outward worth.[13]   10
Doctor   There is means, madam.

1 flags
2 fumitory = fumaria, a type of herb
3 weeds growing on plowed land
4 coarse weed, perhaps burdock
5 poisonous shrub
6 wild flowers blooming when cuckoos are first heard (springtime)
7 wild grass
8 sustaining corn = life-supporting wheat (in British usage, American "corn" = maize)
9 100 men
10 to our eye = before me
11 can man's wisdom = is human wisdom capable of
12 stolen
13 all my outward worth = every *thing* I possess

    Our foster-nurse of nature is repose,

    The which he lacks. That to provoke[14] in him

    Are many simples operative,[15] whose power

    Will close the eye of anguish.[16]

15 *Cordelia*   All blest secrets,

    All you unpublished virtues[17] of the earth,

    Spring with[18] my tears! Be aidant and remediate[19]

    In the good man's distress! Seek, seek for him,

    Lest his ungoverned rage dissolve the life

    That wants the means to lead it.

ENTER MESSENGER

20 *Messenger*   News, madam,

    The British powers are marching hitherward.

    Cordelia   'Tis[20] known before. Our preparation stands

    In expectation of them. O dear father,

    It is thy business that I go about.

25   Therefore great France

    My mourning and important[21] tears hath pitied.

    No blown[22] ambition doth our arms incite,

    But love, dear love, and our aged father's right.

    Soon may I hear and see him!

EXEUNT

---

14 that to provoke = in order to stimulate/arouse that
15 simples (noun) operative (adjective) = herbs/medicines are effective
16 close the eye of anguish = tranquilize
17 unpublished virtues = generally unknown powers
18 spring with = may you grow by means of
19 aidant and remediate (both adjectives) = helpful and curative/remedial
20 it was
21 urgent, importunate
22 (1) blossoming, (2) tainted, inflated

SCENE 5

Gloucester's castle

ENTER REGAN AND OSWALD

Regan   But are my brother's powers set forth?[1]

Oswald   Ay, madam.

Regan   Himself in person there?

Oswald   Madam, with much ado.[2]

Your sister is the better soldier.

Regan   Lord Edmund spake not with your lord at home?

Oswald No, madam.   5

Regan   What might import my sister's letter to him?

Oswald I know not, lady.

Regan   'Faith, he is posted hence[3] on serious matter.

It was great ignorance, Gloucester's eyes being out,

To let him live. Where he arrives he moves   10

All hearts against us. Edmund I think is gone,

In pity of his misery, to dispatch

His nighted life.[4] Moreover, to descry[5]

The strength o' the enemy.

Oswald I must needs after him, madam, with my letter.   15

Regan   Our troops set forth tomorrow, stay with us.

The ways are dangerous.

Oswald   I may not, madam.

My lady charged my duty in this business.

---

1 set forth = on their way
2 (1) fussing about, (2) difficulty
3 away from here
4 his nighted life = Gloucester's darkened/blackened life
5 moreover, to descry = and in addition to discover/examine

Regan   Why should she write to Edmund? Might not you
20   Transport her purposes by word? Belike,[6]
      Something – I know not what: I'll love thee much,[7]
      Let me unseal the letter.
Oswald   Madam, I had rather –
Regan   I know your lady does not love her husband,
      I am sure of that. And at her late being here
25   She gave strange oeillades[8] and most speaking looks
      To noble Edmund. I know you are of her bosom.
Oswald   I, madam?
Regan   I speak in understanding.[9] Y' are. I know't,
      Therefore I do advise you, take this note.[10]
30   My lord is dead. Edmund and I have talked,
      And more convenient[11] is he for my hand
      Than for your lady's. You may gather[12] more.
      If you do find him, pray you give him this,
      And when your mistress hears thus much from you,
35   I pray desire[13] her call[14] her wisdom to her.
      So fare you well.
      If you do chance to hear of that blind traitor,
      Preferment[15] falls on him that cuts him off.

6 perhaps, possibly
7 i.e., if you cooperate with me
8 amorous glances
9 in understanding = from knowledge
10 i.e., her own letter to Edmund
11 befitting, appropriate
12 infer, deduce
13 ask
14 summon, rouse
15 advancement, promotion

Oswald Would I could meet him, madam, I should show
    What party I do follow.
Regan   Fare thee well.   40

EXEUNT

SCENE 6

Fields near Dover

ENTER GLOUCESTER AND EDGAR

Gloucester When shall we come to the top of that same hill?

Edgar You do climb up it now. Look how we labor.

Gloucester Methinks the ground is even.

Edgar Horrible steep.

Hark, do you hear the sea?

Gloucester No, truly.

5 *Edgar* Why then your other senses grow imperfect

By[1] your eyes' anguish.

Gloucester So may it be indeed.

Methinks thy voice is altered, and thou speak'st

In better phrase[2] and matter than thou didst.

Edgar You're much deceived. In nothing am I changed

But in my garments.

10 *Gloucester* Methinks you're better spoken.[3]

Edgar Come on sir, here's the place. Stand still. How fearful

And dizzy 'tis, to cast one's eyes so low!

The crows and choughs[4] that wing the midway air

Show scarce so gross[5] as beetles. Halfway down

15 Hangs one[6] that gathers sampire.[7] Dreadful[8] trade!

Methinks he seems no bigger than his head.

1 because of
2 language, diction
3 you're better spoken = your speech is better
4 crowlike birds (CHUFFS)
5 show scarce so gross = look hardly as big
6 someone, a person
7 aromatic plant, the leaves of which were used in pickling
8 terrifying, formidable, dangerous

The fishermen that walk upon the beach
Appear like mice. And yond tall anchoring bark,[9]
Diminished to her cock,[10] her cock[11] a buoy
Almost too small for sight. The murmuring surge,[12]   20
That on the unnumbered idle pebble chafes,[13]
Cannot be heard so high. I'll look no more,
Lest my brain turn, and the deficient[14] sight
Topple[15] down headlong.

Gloucester   Set me where you stand.

Edgar   Give me your hand. You are now within a foot   25
Of the extreme verge.[16] For all beneath the moon
Would I not leap upright.[17]

Gloucester   Let go my hand.
Here, friend, 's another purse, in it a jewel
Well worth a poor man's taking. Fairies and gods
Prosper it with[18] thee. Go thou farther off,   30
Bid me farewell, and let me hear thee going.

Edgar   Now fare you well, good sir.

Gloucester   With all my heart.

Edgar   Why I do trifle[19] thus with his despair
Is done to cure it.

Gloucester   (*kneeling*) O you mighty gods!

9 ship
10 a ship's small boat, cock-boat
11 her cock = and her cock seems like
12 swell, waves
13 unnumbered idle pebble chafes = uncounted inactive pebbles fret/rub
14 the deficient = my defective/failing
15 topple me
16 extreme verge = outermost limits/bounds
17 leap upright = jump into the air
18 prosper it with = make it do well for
19 why I do trifle = my reason for deluding/tricking/toying with

35   This world I do renounce, and in your sights
        Shake patiently my great affliction off.
        If I could bear it longer, and not fall
        To quarrel[20] with your great opposeless[21] wills,
        My snuff[22] and loathèd part of nature should
40   Burn itself out. If Edgar live, O bless him.
        Now fellow, fare thee well.

Edgar   Gone[23] sir. Farewell.

GLOUCESTER FALLS FORWARD

        (*aside*) And yet I know not how conceit[24] may rob
        The treasury of life, when life itself
        Yields to the theft. Had he been where he thought,
45   By this had thought been past.[25] Alive or dead?
        (*aloud*) Ho, you sir! Friend, hear you sir, speak!
        Thus might he pass[26] indeed. Yet he revives.
        What[27] are you, sir?[28]

Gloucester   Away, and let me die.

Edgar   Hadst thou been aught but gossamer,[29] feathers, air,
50   So many fathom down precipitating,[30]

---

20 fall to quarrel = sink/succumb to disputing/challenging
21 unopposable
22 partially burned out candlewick
23 I'm going, I'm gone
24 how conceit = if fancy/imagination
25 by this thought had been past = (1) by this time (2) because of this, all
    thought would have been over
26 have departed/gone/died
27 how
28 N.B.: Edgar here pretends to be a passerby/a new and different person
29 something light as cobwebs
30 falling headlong

Thou'dst shivered[31] like an egg. But thou dost breathe,
Hast heavy[32] substance, bleed'st not, speak'st, art sound.[33]
Ten masts at each[34] make not the altitude
Which thou hast perpendicularly fell.
Thy life's a miracle. Speak yet again.   55

Gloucester But have I fall'n, or no?

Edgar   From the dread summit of this chalky bourn.[35]
Look up a-height,[36] the shrill-gorged[37] lark so far
Cannot be seen or heard. Do but look up.

Gloucester Alack, I have no eyes.   60
Is wretchedness deprived that benefit
To end itself by death? 'Twas yet some comfort,
When misery could beguile the tyrant's[38] rage,
And frustrate his proud will.

Edgar   Give me your arm.
Up, so. How is 't? Feel you your legs? You stand.   65

Gloucester Too well, too well.

Edgar   This is above all strangeness.
Upon the crown o' the cliff, what thing was that
Which parted from you?

Gloucester   A poor unfortunate beggar.

Edgar   As I stood here below, methought his eyes
Were two full moons. He had a thousand noses,   70

31 shattered
32 an abundance of
33 uninjured
34 (?) end to end?
35 boundary point (of England)
36 on high
37 throated
38 (?) a specific tyrant (Cornwall?) or tyrants generally?

Horns whelked[39] and waved like the enragèd sea.
It was some fiend. Therefore thou happy father,[40]
Think that the clearest[41] gods, who make them honors
Of men's impossibilities,[42] have preserved thee.

75 *Gloucester* I do remember now.[43] Henceforth I'll bear
Affliction till it do cry out itself
"Enough, enough," and die. That thing you speak of,
I took it for a man. Often 'twould say
"The fiend, the fiend." He led me to that place.

80 *Edgar* Bear free and patient thoughts. But who comes here?

ENTER KING LEAR, FANTASTICALLY ADORNED
WITH WILDFLOWERS

The safer sense[44] will ne'er accommodate[45]
His master thus.

Lear No, they cannot touch[46] me for crying. I am the King
himself.

85 *Edgar* O thou side-piercing sight!

Lear Nature's above art in that respect. There's your press-
money.[47] That fellow handles his bow like a crow-keeper.[48]

---

39 horns whelked = he had horns that were twisted/convoluted
40 old man
41 (1) most brightly shining/lustrous, (2) illustrious
42 make them honors of men's impossibilities = create honors for/to
   themselves by performing miracles
43 do remember now = have once again the faculty of memory
44 healthier mind
45 (?) (1) deck himself out (if the reference is exclusively to Lear) (2) be
   reconciled to (if the reference is to Edgar seeing the king like this; "master"
   strongly suggests this latter alternative, as does Edgar's next speech)
46 (?) hit? harm? lay hands on? interfere with?
47 military enlistment bonus
48 scarecrow? person hired to throw rocks at crows?

Draw me[49] a clothier's yard. Look, look, a mouse! Peace,
peace, this piece of toasted[50] cheese will do 't. There's my
gauntlet,[51] I'll prove it on a giant. Bring up the brown bills.[52]   90
O well flown, bird![53] I' the clout,[54] i' the clout. Hewgh![55]
Give the word.[56]

Edgar   Sweet marjoram.[57]

Lear   Pass.[58]

Gloucester I know that voice.   95

Lear   Ha! Goneril with a white beard? They flattered me
like a dog, and told me I had the white hairs in my beard, ere
the black ones were there. To say "ay" and "no" to everything
that I said. "Ay," and "no" too, was no good divinity.[59] When
the rain came to wet me once, and the wind to make me[60]   100
chatter, when the thunder would not peace at my bidding,
there I found 'em, there I smelt 'em out. Go to, they are not
men o' their words, they told me I was everything. 'Tis a lie, I
am not ague-proof.[61]

Gloucester The trick[62] of that voice I do well remember: 105
Is 't not the King?

---

49 draw me = pull back the bow string a full yard
50 browned by fire
51 steel-reinforced glove, worn by knights
52 brown bills = spear/battle-ax weapon, painted brown
53 well flown, bird = good shot, arrow (?) (well flown: falconer's approving cry)
54 archery target
55 whistle-like sound
56 password
57 aromatic herb (MARGEorum)
58 you may pass
59 theology (i.e., it did not make Lear a god)
60 my teeth
61 ague = an acute fever (EYGyou)
62 quality, habit, ways

Lear   Ay, every inch a king.

When I do stare, see how the subject quakes.

I pardon that man's life. What was thy cause?

Adultery?

110   Thou shalt not die. Die for adultery? No,

The wren goes to 't, and the small gilded fly

Does lecher[63] in my sight.

Let copulation thrive, for Gloucester's bastard son

Was kinder to his father than my daughters

115   Got 'tween the lawful sheets.

To 't, luxury,[64] pell-mell,[65] for I lack soldiers.

Behold yond simpering dame,[66]

Whose face between her forks presages snow,[67]

That minces[68] virtue, and does shake the head

120   To hear of pleasure's name.

The fitchew,[69] nor the soilèd[70] horse, goes to 't

With a more riotous[71] appetite.

Down from the waist they[72] are centaurs,[73]

Though women all above.

125   But to the girdle[74] do the gods inherit,[75]

63 sexually indulge ("copulate")
64 lascivious
65 hand to hand, at close quarters, indiscriminately
66 simpering dame = affected/mincing lady
67 (?) forks = legs; the general sense is plainly obscene, but the exact meaning is
   unclear
68 she that disparages/makes little of
69 the fitchew = neither the polecat
70 (?) dirty? overfed?
71 dissolute, wanton, extravagant
72 women
73 top half human, bottom half horse, and notoriously lecherous
74 but to the girdle = only to the belt
75 possess

Beneath is all the fiends'.

There's hell, there's darkness, there is the sulphurous pit,

Burning, scalding, stench, consumption.[76]

Fie, fie, fie! Pah, pah!

Give me an ounce of civet,[77]   130

Good apothecary,[78] to sweeten my imagination.[79]

There's money for thee.

Gloucester   O, let me kiss that hand!

Lear   Let me wipe it first, it smells of mortality.

Gloucester O ruined piece of nature! This great world

Shall so[80] wear out to nought. Dost thou know me?   135

Lear   I remember thine eyes well enough. Dost thou

squiny[81] at me? No, do thy worst, blind Cupid,[82] I'll not love.

Read thou this challenge, mark but the penning[83] of it.

Gloucester Were all the letters suns, I could not see one.[84]

Edgar   (*aside*) I would not take this from report.[85] It is,   140

And my heart breaks at it.

Lear   Read.

Gloucester What, with the case of eyes?[86]

Lear   O ho, are you there with me?[87] No eyes in your head,

nor no money in your purse? Your eyes are in a heavy case,   145

76 conSUMPteeOWN
77 musk scent, derived from civets
78 druggist (aPOtheCAry)
79 anticipation, fancy ("mental image")
80 thus, in this way
81 look slantingly/sideways, as might a whore ("squint")
82 Cupid was often portrayed as blind
83 writing, handwriting
84 "one": Quarto
85 take this from report = accept/believe this if it were rumored
86 case of eyes = empty eye sockets
87 i.e., so that's it, that's what you mean

your purse in a light, yet you see how this world goes.

Gloucester I see it feelingly.[88]

Lear What, art mad?[89] A man may see how this world goes
with no eyes. Look with thine ears. See how yond justice rails
150 upon[90] yond simple thief. Hark in thine ear.[91] Change places
and, handy-dandy,[92] which is the justice, which is the thief?
Thou hast seen a farmer's dog bark at a beggar?

Gloucester Ay, sir.

Lear And the creature[93] run from the cur? There thou
155 mightst behold the great image of authority: a dog's obeyed
in office.

Thou rascal beadle,[94] hold thy bloody hand![95]

Why dost thou lash[96] that whore? Strip thine own back.

Thou hotly lusts to use her in that kind[97]
160 For which thou whipp'st her. The usurer hangs the
cozener.[98]

Through tattered clothes small vices do appear.

Robes and furred gowns hide all.[99] Plate[100] sin with gold,

And the strong lance of justice hurtless[101] breaks.

---

88 (1) with understanding, from experience, (2) appropriately, (3) with great
 emotion
89 i.e., how can you perceive the world via the sense of touch?
90 justice rails upon = magistrate / judge ("justice of the peace") abuses
91 hark in thine ear = listen
92 handy-dandy = take your pick (from the children's game)
93 man
94 under-bailiff / sheriff
95 hold thy . . . hand = stop
96 whip (whipping was a common punishment)
97 manner, fashion, way
98 cheat, deceiver, impostor★
99 i.e., all vices, large as well as small
100 overlay
101 causing no harm / injury

Arm it[102] in rags, a pigmy's straw does pierce it.   165
None does offend, none, I say, none, I'll able[103] 'em.
Take that of me, my friend, who have the power
To seal th' accuser's lips. Get thee glass eyes,
And like a scurvy politician,[104] seem
To see the things thou dost not. Now, now, now, now.   170
Pull off my boots. Harder, harder. So.

Edgar   O matter and impertinency[105] mixed,
Reason in madness!

Lear   · If thou wilt weep[106] my fortunes, take my eyes.
I know thee well enough, thy name is Gloucester.   175
Thou must be patient, we[107] came crying hither.
Thou know'st, the first time that we smell the air,
We wawl[108] and cry. I will preach to thee. Mark.

Gloucester Alack, alack the day!

Lear   When we are born, we cry that we are come   180
To this great stage of fools. This a good block.[109]
It were a delicate[110] stratagem, to shoe
A troop of horse[111] with felt. I'll put 't in proof,
And when I have stol'n upon these son-in-laws,
Then kill, kill, kill, kill, kill, kill!   185

ENTER ATTENDANTS

102 sin
103 vouch for, warrant
104 scurvy politician = contemptible/worthless schemer/plotter
105 irrelevancy (imPERtiNENsee)
106 wilt weep = wish/want to weep for
107 N.B.: the royal "we" appears, and then disappears again
108 loud/harsh cry
109 (?) log/tree stump, real or imagined?
110 charming, pleasant, delightful, sumptuous
111 of horse = cavalry

Attendant O here he is. Lay hand upon him. Sir,
  Your most dear daughter –

Lear   No rescue? What, a prisoner? I am even[112]
  The natural[113] fool of fortune. Use me well,

190 You shall have ransom. Let me have surgeons,[114]
  I am cut[115] to the brains.

Attendant   You shall have anything.

Lear   No seconds?[116] All[117] myself?
  Why, this would make a man a man of salt,[118]
  To use his eyes for garden water-pots.

195 I will die bravely, like a smug[119] bridegroom.
  What? I will be jovial.[120] Come, come,
  I am a king, masters,[121] know you that?

Attendant You are a royal one, and we obey you.

Lear   Then there's life in't. Come, and[122] you get it,

200 You shall get it with running. Sa, sa, sa, sa.

EXIT LEAR RUNNING

Attendant A sight most pitiful in the meanest wretch,
  Past speaking of in a king. Thou hast a daughter,[123]

112 uniformly, regularly
113 born
114 doctors, medical men
115 wounded, distressed
116 others, followers/supporters
117 only
118 man of salt = a man who cries
119 sleek, complacent, consciously respectable
120 majestic ("Jove-like")
121 misters, fellows
122 if
123 Cordelia

Who redeems nature from the general[124] curse

Which twain[125] have brought her[126] to.

Edgar   Hail, gentle sir.

Attendant Sir, speed you. What's your will?[127]   205

Edgar   Do you hear aught, sir, of a battle toward?

Attendant Most sure and vulgar.[128]

Everyone hears that, which can distinguish sound.

Edgar   But by your favor,[129] how near's the other army?

Attendant Near and on speedy foot. The main descry[130]   210

Stands on the hourly thought.[131]

Edgar   I thank you, sir, that's all.

Attendant Though that the Queen on special cause is here,

Her army is moved on.

Edgar   I thank you, sir.

EXIT ATTENDANT

Gloucester You ever-gentle gods, take my breath from me,

Let not my worser spirit tempt me again   215

To die before you please.

Edgar   Well pray you, father.

Gloucester Now, good sir, what are you?

---

124 widespread (this has been taken to refer to the curse brought on all men's
    heads by Adam and Eve, the original "twain," but since the curse here is
    what the "twain have brought to her," i.e., to Cordelia, the broader
    religious reference seems inapplicable)
125 two daughters (Goneril and Regan)
126 Cordelia
127 what's your will = what is your wish, what can I do for you
128 current, prevalent
129 by your favor = if you please
130 final perception / observation
131 stands on the hourly thought = is expected at any hour

Edgar   A most poor man, made tame to fortune's blows,
Who by the art[132] of known and feeling sorrows,
220   Am pregnant[133] to good pity. Give me your hand,
I'll lead you to some biding.[134]
Gloucester   Hearty thanks.
The bounty[135] and the benison of heaven
To boot, and boot!

ENTER OSWALD

Oswald   A proclaimed[136] prize. Most happy!
That eyeless head of thine was first framed flesh
225   To raise my fortunes. Thou old unhappy traitor,
Briefly thyself remember.[137] The sword is out
That must destroy thee.
Gloucester   Now let thy friendly hand
Put strength enough to't.[138]

EDGAR INTERPOSES

Oswald   Wherefore, bold peasant,
Darest thou support a published traitor? Hence,
230   Lest that th' infection of his fortune take
Like[139] hold on thee. Let go his arm.
Edgar   (*in country dialect*) Ch'ill[140] not let go, zir, without

132 practical skill
133 ready, apt
134 dwelling, residence
135 generosity, gift
136 PROclaimed
137 think of, commemorate
138 into it
139 similar, the same
140 I will

vurther 'casion.[141]

Oswald Let go, slave, or thou diest!

Edgar Good gentleman, go your gait,[142] and let poor volk   235
pass. An chud ha' bin zwaggered[143] out of my life, 'twould
not ha' bin zo long as 'tis by a vortnight. Nay, come not near
th' old man. Keep out, che vor[144] ye, or ise[145] try whether
your costard[146] or my ballow[147] be the harder. Ch'ill[148] be
plain with you.   240

Oswald Out, dunghill!

Edgar Ch'ill pick[149] your teeth, zir. Come,[150] no matter vor
your foins.[151]

THEY FIGHT, OSWALD FALLS

Oswald Slave, thou hast slain me. Villain, take my purse.
If ever thou wilt[152] thrive, bury my body,   245
And give the letters which thou find'st about me
To Edmund Earl of Gloucester. Seek him out
Upon[153] the British[154] party. O untimely death, death.

DIES

141 vurther 'casion = further occasion ("consideration, reason, ground")
142 way
143 an chud ha' bin zwaggered = if I could have been blustered/swaggered
144 che vor = I warrant/promise/warn
145 I shall
146 head ("large apple")
147 staff, cudgel
148 I'll be
149 break
150 come on
151 vor your foins = about your sword thrusts/strokes
152 wish to
153 in
154 i.e., as opposed to the French (Cordelia's)

Edgar   I know thee well. A serviceable[155] villain,

250   As duteous[156] to the vices of thy mistress

As badness would desire.

Gloucester   What, is he dead?

Edgar   Sit you down, father. Rest you.

Let's see these pockets,[157] the letters that he speaks of

May be my friends. He's dead, I am only sorry

255   He had no other deathsman.[158] Let us see.

Leave, gentle wax,[159] and manners, blame us not.

To know our enemies' minds, we rip their hearts,

Their papers is more lawful.

READS

"Let our reciprocal vows be remembered. You have many

260   opportunities to cut him off.[160] If your will want not, time

and place will be fruitfully offered. There is nothing done.[161]

If he return the conqueror, then am I the prisoner, and his

bed my jail, from the loathèd warmth whereof deliver me,

and supply[162] the place for your labor.[163]

265   "Your (wife, so I would[164] say) affectionate servant,

Goneril."

O undistinguished space[165] of woman's will!

155 diligent, subservient (SERviSAble)
156 obedient
157 pouches, small bags
158 executioner
159 leave, gentle wax = your leave / permission, noble sealing wax
160 cut him off = kill Albany
161 (?) down = down on paper, written down
162 fill
163 a sexual reference
164 wish to
165 undistinguished space = distinctionless dimensions

A plot upon her virtuous husband's life,
And the exchange my brother! Here in the sands,
Thee[166] I'll rake up,[167] the post[168] unsanctified   270
Of murderous lechers. And in the mature[169] time
With this ungracious paper strike the sight[170]
Of the death-practiced[171] Duke. For him 'tis well
That of thy death and business I can tell.

Gloucester   The king is mad. How stiff is my vile sense,[172]   275
That I stand up, and have ingenious[173] feeling
Of my huge sorrows! Better I were distract,[174]
So should my thoughts be severed from my griefs,
And woes by wrong imaginations lose
The knowledge of themselves.

Edgar   Give me your hand.   280

DISTANT DRUMMING

Far off methinks I hear the beaten drum.
Come father, I'll bestow you with a friend.

EXEUNT

166 Oswald
167 rake up = cover
168 rapid messenger
169 ripe
170 strike the sight = assault the eyes
171 death-practiced = intended/plotted to be killed
172 stiff is my vile sense = how resolute/firm/steadfast are my despicable
organs of perception
173 capable, functional
174 confused, perplexed, mentally scattered

SCENE 7

A tent in the French camp, Lear on a bed asleep

SOFT MUSIC

ENTER CORDELIA, KENT, AND DOCTOR

5   *Cordelia* O thou good Kent, how shall I live and work
       To match thy goodness? My life will be too short,
       And every measure[1] fail me.

  Kent   To be acknowledged, madam, is[2] o'erpaid.
       All my reports go with[3] the modest truth,
       Nor more, nor clipped,[4] but so.

  Cordelia   Be better suited,[5]

10   These weeds[6] are memories of those worser hours.
       I prithee, put them off.

15 *Kent*   Pardon, dear madam,
       Yet to be known shortens my made[7] intent.
       My boon[8] I make it that you know[9] me not
       Till time and I think meet.

  Cordelia   Then be't so, my good lord.
       (*to Doctor*) How does the King?

  Doctor   Madam, sleeps still.

  Cordelia O you kind gods,

1 course of action
2 is to be
3 go with = are part of/match/accompany
4 cut, reduced
5 dressed
6 clothes
7 planned, contrived
8 petition, request
9 recognize

Cure this great breach in his abusèd[10] nature.
The untuned and jarring[11] senses, O wind up,[12]
Of this child-changed[13] father!

Doctor   So please your Majesty   20
That we may wake the King. He hath slept long.

Cordelia   Be governed by your knowledge, and proceed
I' the sway of your own will. Is he arrayed?[14]

Attendant Ay, madam. In the heaviness of his sleep
We put fresh garments on him.

Doctor   Be by,[15] good madam, when we do awake him,
I doubt of his temperance.[16]   25

ENTER LEAR, IN A CHAIR CARRIED BY SERVANTS

Cordelia   O my dear father, restoration[17] hang
Thy medicine on my lips, and let this kiss
Repair those violent harms that my two sisters
Have in thy reverence[18] made.

Kent   Kind and dear princess.   30

Cordelia   (*to Lear*) Had you not been their father, these white
flakes[19]
Had challenged[20] pity of them. Was this a face

10 violated, worn out
11 discordant, clashing
12 wind up = repair, tighten, re-tune
13 changed by the actions of his children
14 clothed, dressed
15 near
16 rational self-restraint
17 recovery
18 thy reverence = your reverenced self
19 tufts (of hair)
20 demanded

To be opposed against²¹ the warring winds?
35 Mine enemy's dog, though he had bit me,
Should have stood that night against²² my fire.
And wast thou fain (poor father)
To hovel thee with swine and rogues forlorn,²³
In short²⁴ and musty straw? Alack, alack,
40 'Tis wonder that thy life and wits at once
Had not concluded all. He wakes, speak to him.

Doctor Madam, do you, 'tis fittest.

Cordelia How does my royal lord? How fares your Majesty?

Lear You do me wrong to take me out o' the grave.
Thou art a soul in bliss, but I am bound
45 Upon a wheel of fire, that²⁵ mine own tears
Do scald like molten lead.

Cordelia   Sir, do you know me?

Lear You are a spirit, I know. Where did you die?

Cordelia Still, still, far wide!²⁶

50 *Doctor* He's scarce awake, let him alone awhile.

Lear Where have I been? Where am I? Fair daylight?
I am mightily abused, I should e'en²⁷ die with pity
To see another thus.²⁸ I know not what to say.
I will not swear these are my hands. Let's see,
I feel this pin prick. Would I were assured

21 opposed against = confronted with
22 directly facing
23 depraved
24 i.e., stiff and prickly, without the resilience of longer straw
25 so that
26 off, away
27 quite, fully
28 another thus = someone else in the state I'm in

  Of my condition.

Cordelia   O look upon me, sir,

  And hold your hands in benediction o'er me.

  You must not kneel.

Lear   Pray, do not mock me.

  I am a very foolish fond old man,   55

  Fourscore and upward, not an hour more, nor less.

  And to deal plainly,

  I fear I am not in my perfect mind.

  Methinks I should know you, and know this man,

  Yet I am doubtful. For I am mainly[29] ignorant   60

  What place this is. And all the skill[30] I have

  Remembers not these garments. Nor I know not

  Where I did lodge last night. Do not laugh at me,

  For (as I am a man) I think this lady

  To be my child Cordelia.

Cordelia   And so I am. I am.   65

Lear Be your tears wet? Yes, 'faith. I pray, weep not.

  If you have poison for me, I will drink it.

  I know you do not love me, for your sisters

  Have (as I do remember) done me wrong.

  You have some cause, they have not.

Cordelia   No cause, no cause.   70

Lear Am I in France?

Kent   In your own kingdom, sir.

Lear Do not abuse me.

Doctor Be comforted good madam, the great rage

---

29 entirely
30 reason, mental faculties

You see is killed in him. Desire him to go in,

75   Trouble him no more till further settling.

Cordelia Will't please your Highness walk?

Lear   You must bear with

me.

Pray you now, forget and forgive,

I am old and foolish.

EXEUNT

Act 5

SCENE I

The British camp, near Dover

ENTER, WITH DRUM AND COLORS, EDMUND, REGAN,
ATTENDANTS, AND SOLDIERS

Edmund (*to Attendant*) Know of[1] the Duke if his last purpose
   hold,
   Or whether, since, he is[2] advised by aught
   To change the course. He's full of alteration
   And self-reproving. Bring[3] his constant pleasure.[4]

EXIT ATTENDANT

Regan   Our sister's man is certainly miscarried.[5]   5
Edmund 'Tis to be doubted,[6] madam.
Regan   Now sweet lord,

1 know of = find out from
2 has been
3 fetch/bring me
4 constant pleasure = firm choice
5 gone astray
6 feared

You know the goodness[7] I intend upon you.

Tell me but truly, but then speak the truth,

Do you not love my sister?

Edmund   In honored[8] love.

10 *Regan*   But have you never found my brother's way

To the forfended[9] place?[10]

Edmund No, by mine honor, madam.

Regan   I never shall endure[11] her. Dear my lord

Be not familiar[12] with her.

Edmund   Fear not.

ENTER, WITH DRUM AND COLORS, ALBANY,
GONERIL, AND SOLDIERS

15 She and the Duke her husband.

Goneril   (*aside*) I had rather lose the battle than that sister

Should loosen[13] him and me.

Albany   Our very loving sister, well be-met.

Sir, this I heard, the King is come to his daughter,

20 With others, whom the rigor[14] of our state

Forced to cry out.

Regan   Why is this reasoned?

Goneril   (*to Albany*) Combine together 'gainst the enemy,

For these domestic and particular broils

Are not the question here.

---

7 benefit, advantage, good fortune
8 dignified, respectful
9 prohibited, forbidden
10 i.e., have you had sex with her
11 tolerate, bear, suffer
12 intimate, free
13 detach, make a breach between
14 severity, harshness

Albany	Let's then determine

With the ancient of war[15] on our proceedings.   25

Edmund I shall attend you presently at your tent.

Regan   Sister, you'll go with us?

Goneril   No.

Regan   'Tis most convenient,[16] pray go with us.

Goneril   (aside) O ho, I know the riddle.[17] (aloud) I will go.   30

EXEUNT REGAN AND GONERIL

ENTER EDGAR, IN PEASANT DISGUISE

Edgar   (to Albany) If e'er your Grace had speech with man so poor,

Hear me one word.

Albany   (to Soldiers) I'll overtake you. (to Edgar)
Speak.

EXEUNT SOLDIERS

Edgar   Before you fight the battle, ope this letter.

If you have victory, let the trumpet sound

For[18] him that brought it. Wretched though I seem,   35

I can produce a champion[19] that will prove[20]

What is avouchèd there. If you miscarry,[21]

---

15 the ancient of war = those with more military experience (ancient: a plural noun, here)
16 appropriate, suitable
17 i.e., Regan wants to protect her own interest in Edmund, and watch her sister
18 to call
19 i.e., a man who will represent, in combat, what Edgar maintains
20 put to trial by combat
21 fail, die

Your business of the world hath so[22] an end,

And machination ceases. Fortune love you.

Albany   Stay till I have read the letter.

40 *Edgar*   I was forbid it.

When time shall serve,[23] let but the herald cry,

And I'll appear again.

Albany   Why, fare thee well, I will o'erlook thy paper.

EXIT EDGAR

ENTER EDMUND

Edmund The enemy's in view, draw up[24] your powers.

45 Here is the guess of their true strength and forces

By diligent discovery; but your haste

Is now urged on you.

Albany   We will greet[25] the time.

EXIT ALBANY

Edmund To both these sisters have I sworn my love,

Each jealous of[26] the other as the stung

50 Are of the adder. Which of them shall I take?

Both? One? Or neither? Neither can be enjoyed,

If both remain alive. To take the widow

Exasperates,[27] makes mad her sister Goneril,

And hardly[28] shall I carry out my side,

22 thus
23 be advantageous/useful/favorable/suitable
24 draw up = put in proper combat array
25 deal with, address, receive
26 jealous of = furious at
27 embitters, enrages
28 uneasily, painfully

Her[29] husband being alive. Now then we'll use   55
His countenance[30] for the battle, which being done
Let her who would be rid of him devise
His speedy taking off. As for his mercy
Which he intends to Lear and to Cordelia,
The battle done, and they within our power,   60
Shall[31] never see his pardon, for my state
Stands on me to defend, not to debate.

EXIT

29 Goneril's
30 (1) patronage, support, (2) appearance, dignity, position
31 they shall

SCENE 2

A field between the two camps

ALARUM WITHIN. ENTER, WITH DRUM AND COLORS,
LEAR, CORDELIA, AND SOLDIERS, WHO ALL CROSS
THE STAGE AND THEN EXEUNT

ENTER EDGAR AND GLOUCESTER

Edgar   Here, father, take the shadow of this tree
For your good host. Pray that the right may thrive.[1]
If ever I return to you again,
I'll bring you comfort.
Gloucester   Grace go with you, sir!

EXIT EDGAR

ALARUM AND RETREAT WITHIN

ENTER EDGAR

5 *Edgar*   Away, old man, give me thy hand, away!
King Lear hath lost, he and his daughter ta'en,
Give me thy hand. Come on.
Gloucester No further, sir, a man may rot even here.
Edgar   What, in ill thoughts again? Men must endure
10   Their going hence, even as their coming hither.
Ripeness is all. Come on.
Gloucester   And that's true too.

EXEUNT

1 prosper, be successful

SCENE 3

The British camp near Dover

ENTER TRIUMPHANT, WITH DRUM AND COLORS,
EDMUND, WITH LEAR AND CORDELIA AS PRISONERS,
AND WITH CAPTAIN,[1] SOLDIERS, ETC.

Edmund Some officers[2] take them away. Good guard,[3]
    Until their greater[4] pleasures first be known
    That[5] are to censure[6] them.

Cordelia   We are not the first
    Who with best meaning have incurred the worst.
    (*to Lear*) For thee oppressèd king I am cast down,   5
    Myself could else out-frown false fortune's frown.
    (*to Edmund*) Shall we not see these daughters and these
    sisters?

Lear   No, no, no, no! Come let's away to prison,
    We two alone will sing like birds i' the cage.
    When thou dost ask me blessing, I'll kneel down   10
    And ask of thee forgiveness. So we'll live,
    And pray, and sing, and tell old tales, and laugh
    At gilded butterflies.[7] And hear poor rogues
    Talk of court news, and we'll talk with them too,
    Who loses and who wins, who's in, who's out,   15
    And take upon's the mystery of things,

---

1 subordinate officer
2 subordinates
3 good guard = keep good guard of them
4 superior, higher-ranking
5 those who are
6 judge
7 gilded butterflies = fashionable vain/gaudily dressed people/courtiers

As if we were God's spies. And we'll wear out,[8]
In a walled prison, packs and sects[9] of great ones,
That ebb and flow by the moon.

Edmund   Take them away.

20 **Lear**   Upon such sacrifices,[10] my Cordelia,
The gods themselves throw incense. Have I caught[11] thee?
He that parts us shall bring a brand[12] from heaven,
And fire[13] us hence, like foxes. Wipe thine eyes,
The good years shall devour them, flesh and fell,[14]
25 Ere they shall make us weep.
We'll see 'em starve first. Come.

EXEUNT LEAR AND CORDELIA, GUARDED

Edmund Come hither, captain, hark.
Take thou this note, go follow them to prison.
One step I have advanced[15] thee. If thou dost
30 As this instructs thee, thou dost make thy way
To noble[16] fortunes. Know thou this, that men
Are as the time is, to be tender-minded
Does not become a sword. Thy great employment[17]
Will not bear question.[18] Either say thou'lt do 't,

---

8 wear out = outlast
9 packs and sects = gangs/collections and partisans/followers
10 i.e., in the "pagan" sense: the killing of people or animals as sacrificial objects
11 ensnared, gotten to
12 stick of burning wood
13 drive
14 skin, hide
15 step . . . advanced = promoted ("moved forward/upward")
16 great, distinguished
17 profession, occupation
18 inquiry, discussion

Or thrive by other means.

Captain   I'll do 't, my lord.   35

Edmund About it,[19] and write happy[20] when thou hast done.

    Mark,[21] I say instantly; and carry it[22] so

    As I have set it down.

Captain I cannot draw a cart, nor eat dried oats,

    If it be man's work, I'll do 't.[23]   40

EXIT CAPTAIN

FLOURISH

ENTER ALBANY, GONERIL, REGAN,
CAPTAIN 2, AND SOLDIERS

Albany (*to Edmund*) Sir, you have showed today your valiant
    strain,[24]

    And fortune led you well. You have the captives

    That were the opposites of this day's strife.

    I do require them of you, so to use them

    As we shall find their merits and our safety   45

    May equally determine.

Edmund   Sir, I thought it fit

    To send the old and miserable King

    To some retention[25] and appointed guard,

    Whose age had charms in it, whose title more,

---

19 about it = do it, set about it
20 fortunate, lucky
21 note
22 carry it = carry it out
23 captain's speech: from Quarto
24 capacity, effort
25 confinement, detention

50   To pluck the common bosom[26] on his side,

         And turn our impressed lances[27] in our eyes

         Which[28] do command them. With him I sent the Queen,

         My reason all the same, and they are ready

         Tomorrow, or at further space,[29] t' appear

         Where you shall hold your session.

55 *Albany*   Sir, by your patience,[30]

         I hold you but a subject of[31] this war,

         Not as a brother.[32]

      Regan   That's as we list[33] to grace him.

         Methinks our pleasure might have been demanded,[34]

         Ere you had spoke so far. He led our powers,

60   Bore the commission[35] of my place and person,

         The which immediacy[36] may well stand up

         And call itself your brother.

      Goneril   Not so hot.

         In his own grace[37] he doth exalt[38] himself,

         More than in your addition.[39]

      Regan   In my rights,

---

26 common bosom = public/general opinion ("heart")
27 impressed lances = forcibly enlisted cavalry soldiers
28 we who
29 time, interval
30 forbearance, permission (politely conventional)
31 subject of = subordinate in
32 a brother = an equal
33 choose, wish
34 requested
35 authority, trust
36 direct connection
37 behavior, honor
38 raise, elevate
39 title, name

By me invested,[40] he compeers[41] the best.   65

Goneril That were the most,[42] if he should husband you.

Regan Jesters do oft prove prophets.

Goneril   Holla, holla!

That eye that told you so looked but a-squint.

Regan Lady, I am not well, else I should answer

From a full-flowing stomach.[43] *(to Edmund)* General,   70

Take thou my soldiers, prisoners, patrimony,[44]

Dispose of them, of me, the walls is thine.[45]

Witness the world, that I create thee here

My lord and master.

Goneril   Mean you to enjoy[46] him?

Albany The let-alone lies not[47] in your good will.   75

Edmund Nor in thine, lord.

Albany   Half-blooded[48] fellow, yes.

Regan   *(to Edmund)* Let the drum strike,[49] and prove[50] my title

thine.[51]

Albany Stay yet, hear reason. Edmund, I arrest thee

---

40 clothed, enveloped
41 rivals, is the equal of
42 the most = most fully/completely
43 full-flowing stomach = intense passion/emotion
44 inheritance from her father
45 the walls is thine = you have conquered the castle (i.e., the body that enc-
   loses her soul, or Regan herself)
46 possess (with sexual overtones)
47 let-alone lies not in = injunction ("power to interfere") is not located in/
   controlled by
48 half-blooded = son of a noble father but a commoner mother, and therefore
   only half-noble
49 be struck/sounded (i.e., in announcement)
50 i.e., by combat
51 has been given to you

On capital treason, and[52] in thine attaint

80   This gilded serpent. (*to Goneril*) For[53] your claim, fair sister,[54]

I bar it in the interest of[55] my wife.

'Tis she is sub-contracted[56] to this lord,

And I her husband contradict[57] your bans.

(*to Edmund*) If you will marry, make your loves[58] to me,

My lady is bespoke.

85   *Goneril*   An interlude![59]

Albany   Thou art armed, Gloucester, let the trumpet sound.

If none appear to prove[60] upon thy head

Thy heinous,[61] manifest, and many treasons,

There is my pledge.[62] (*throws down a glove*) I'll make[63] it on

thy heart,

90   Ere I taste bread, thou[64] art in nothing less

Than I have here proclaimed thee.

Regan   Sick,[65] O sick!

52 and include
53 as for
54 N.B.: Albany distances himself from Goneril by calling her his "sister," which
   prepares for his ironical "protection" of his "wife's interest," in the following
   lines
55 in the interest of = to protect the rights of
56 sub-contracted = engaged to be married again (marriage was and is still, in
   law, a "contract")
57 forbid, oppose (the "banns" are announced in open church, and anyone with
   reason to oppose the proposed marriage has, at that point, the right to halt it)
58 make your loves = propose marriage (!)
59 short play, usually comic (a "farce")
60 in combat (i.e., literally "upon your head")
61 infamous, atrocious
62 promise of combat, signaled by throwing down a gauntlet/glove
63 establish, prove
64 that you
65 I am sick

Goneril   (*aside*) If not,[66] I'll ne'er[67] trust medicine.[68]

Edmund   (*throws down glove*) There's my exchange. What[69] in the
world he is

That names me traitor, villain-like he lies.

Call by the trumpet. He that dares approach,   95

On him, on you, who not,[70] I will maintain

My truth and honor firmly.

Albany   A herald,[71] ho!

Edmund   A herald, ho, a herald!

Albany   Trust to thy single virtue,[72] for thy soldiers,

All levied[73] in my name, have in my name   100

Took their discharge.

Regan   My sickness grows upon me.

Albany   She is not well, convey[74] her to my tent.

EXIT REGAN, ESCORTED

ENTER HERALD

Come hither, herald, let the trumpet sound,

And read out this.

TRUMPET SOUNDS

66 if not = if you're not sick
67 never again
68 drugs ("poison")
69 whatever
70 who not = and who not (i.e., on anyone and everyone)
71 a man who makes proclamations
72 single virtue = solitary power, strength
73 enlisted
74 escort

105 *Herald* (*reads*) "If any man of quality or degree[75] within the
lists[76] of the army will maintain[77] upon Edmund, supposèd
Earl of Gloucester, that he is a manifold[78] traitor, let him
appear by the third sound of the trumpet. He[79] is bold[80] in
his defense."

FIRST TRUMPET CALL

110 *Herald* Again!

SECOND TRUMPET CALL

Herald Again!

THIRD TRUMPET CALL

A TRUMPET ANSWERS WITHIN

ENTER EDGAR, ARMED

Albany Ask him his purposes, why he appears
Upon this call o' the trumpet.
Herald   What are you?[81]
Your name, your quality? And why you answer
This present summons?
115 *Edgar*   Know, my name is[82] lost
By treason's tooth. Bare-gnawn[83] and canker-bit,[84]
Yet am I noble as the adversary

75 quality or degree = rank
76 rolls
77 prosecute
78 many-times-over
79 Edmund
80 fearless
81 WHAT are YOU
82 has been
83 bare bitten away
84 ulcer/insect-eaten

I come to cope.[85]

Albany	Which is that adversary?

Edgar   What's he that speaks for Edmund Earl of Gloucester?

Edmund Himself, what say'st thou to him?

Edgar   Draw thy sword,   120

That[86] if my speech offend a noble heart,

Thy arm may do thee justice. Here is mine.[87]

Behold, it is the privilege of mine honors,

My oath, and my profession.[88] I protest,[89]

Maugre[90] thy strength, youth, place, and eminence,   125

Despite thy victor sword and fire-new[91] fortune,

Thy valor and thy heart, thou art a traitor,

False to thy gods, thy brother, and thy father,

Conspirant 'gainst this high-illustrious prince,[92]

And from th' extremest upward[93] of thy head,   130

To the descent[94] and dust below thy foot,

A most toad-spotted[95] traitor. Say thou "No,"

This sword, this arm, and my best spirits,[96] are bent[97]

To prove upon thy heart, whereto I speak,[98]

85 battle, engage ("fight")
86 so that
87 my sword
88 declaration (proFEseeOWN)
89 solemnly state/affirm
90 in spite of
91 fire-new = newly forged
92 Albany
93 extremest upward = very top
94 lowest part
95 toad-spotted = loathsome
96 best spirits = highest being
97 braced, set
98 whereto I speak = from which (as to himself) and to which (as to Edmund)
   I address myself

Thou[99] liest.

135 *Edmund*   In wisdom I should ask thy name,

But since thy outside looks so fair and warlike,

And that thy tongue some say[100] of breeding breathes,

What safe and nicely[101] I might well delay

By rule of knighthood, I disdain and spurn.

140 Back do I toss these treasons to thy head,

With the hell-hated lie, o'erwhelm[102] thy heart,

Which for[103] they yet glance by and scarcely bruise,[104]

This sword of mine shall give them instant way,[105]

Where they[106] shall rest for ever. Trumpets, speak!

ALARUMS

THEY FIGHT

EDMUND FALLS

Albany (*to Edgar*) Save[107] him, save him!

145 *Goneril*   (*to Edmund*) This is

practice, Gloucester.

By the law of arms thou wast not bound to answer

An unknown opposite. Thou art not vanquished,

But cozened, and beguiled.

Albany   Shut your mouth, dame,

---

99 that thou
100 (1) taste, (2) attempt
101 formally, strictly
102 in order to overwhelm / overturn / tumble down
103 because (i.e., visibly, obviously)
104 injure (i.e., your lying, treasonous heart)
105 instant way = an immediate path / road (to his heart, by piercing right to it)
106 your treasons and lies
107 spare

Or with this paper shall I stop[108] it. (*to Edmund*) Hold,[109] sir.

(*to Goneril*) Thou worse than any name,[110] read thine own   150
evil.

No tearing,[111] lady, I perceive you know it.

Goneril Say if I do, the laws are mine, not thine,

Who can arraign[112] me for't?

EXIT GONERIL

Albany   Most monstrous! O!

(*to Edmund*) Know'st thou this paper?

Edmund   Ask me not what I
know.

Albany   Go after her, she's desperate, govern her.   155

Edmund   What you have charged me with, that have I done,

And more, much more, the time will bring it out.

'Tis past, and so am I. (*to Edgar*) But what art thou

That hast this fortune on[113] me? If thou'rt noble,

I do forgive thee.

Edgar   Let's exchange charity.[114]   160

I am no less in blood than thou art, Edmund.

If[115] more, the more thou hast wronged me.

My name is Edgar, and[116] thy father's son.

---

108 plug, close
109 (?) hold on (stay alive)? just a moment?
110 i.e., any name that he could use to describe her
111 ripping it up
112 indict, charge (i.e., since she rules, she *is* the law)
113 hast this fortune on = made this accident/disaster occur to
114 kindness
115 if I am
116 and I am

The gods are just, and of our pleasant[117] vices

165 Make instruments to plague us.

  The dark and vicious[118] place where thee he got[119]

  Cost him his eyes.

Edmund   Th' hast spoken right, 'tis true,

  The wheel is come full circle, I am here.

Albany (*to Edgar*) Methought thy very gait did prophesy

170 A royal nobleness. I must embrace thee,

  Let sorrow split my heart, if ever I

  Did hate thee or thy father.

Edgar   Worthy prince, I know't.

Albany Where have you hid yourself?

  How have you known the miseries of your father?

175 *Edgar* By nursing them, my lord. List a brief tale,

  And when 'tis told, O that my heart would burst.

  The bloody proclamation to escape,

  That followed me so near (O our lives' sweetness!

  That we the pain of death would hourly die

180 Rather than die at once!) taught me to shift

  Into a madman's rags, t' assume a semblance

  That very[120] dogs disdained. And in this habit

  Met I my father with his bleeding rings,[121]

  Their precious stones[122] new lost. Became[123] his guide,

185 Led him, begged for him, saved him from despair.

---

117 agreeable (i.e., to us)
118 wicked, immoral
119 where thee he got = where you put him
120 the very
121 eye sockets ("circular objects")
122 eyes
123 I became

Never (O fault!) revealed myself unto him,
Until some half-hour past, when I was armed.[124]
Not sure, though hoping of this good success,
I asked his blessing, and from first to last
Told him my pilgrimage. But his flawed[125] heart   190
(Alack too weak the conflict to support)
'Twixt two extremes of passion, joy and grief,
Burst smilingly.

Edmund   This speech of yours hath moved me,
And shall perchance do good, but speak you on,
You look as you had something more to say.   195

Albany   If there be more, more woeful, hold it in,
For I am almost ready to dissolve,[126]
Hearing of this.

ENTER ATTENDANT, WITH A BLOODY KNIFE

Attendant   Help, help. O help!

Edgar   What kind of help?

Albany   Speak, man.

Edgar   What means this bloody knife?

Attendant   'Tis hot, it smokes,   200
It came even from the heart of — O she's dead.

Albany   Who[127] dead? Speak, man.

Attendant   Your lady, sir, your lady. And her sister
By her is poisoned. She confesses it.

Edmund   I was contracted to them both, all three[128]   205

124 wearing armor and bearing weapons
125 broken
126 i.e., into tears
127 who is
128 three of us

Now marry[129] in an instant.

Edgar   Here comes Kent.

Albany   (to Attendants) Produce their bodies, be they alive or
dead.

This judgment of the heavens, that makes us tremble,

Touches us not with pity.

EXIT ATTENDANT

ENTER KENT

                    O is this he?[130]

210   The time will not allow the compliment

Which very[131] manners urges.

Kent   I am come

To bid my king and master aye[132] good night.

Is he not here?

Albany   Great thing of us forgot!

Speak, Edmund, where's the King? And where's Cordelia?

THE BODIES OF GONERIL AND REGAN ARE BROUGHT IN

See'st thou this object,[133] Kent?

215 Kent   Alack, why thus?

Edmund   Yet Edmund was beloved.

The one the other poisoned for my sake,

And after slew herself.

Albany   Even so. Cover their faces.

---

129 unite (i.e., in death)
130 i.e., Kent is still rudely dressed and Albany does not at once know him
131 true
132 forever
133 sight

Edmund I pant for life. Some good I mean to do,
    Despite of[134] mine own nature. Quickly send   220
    (Be brief in it) to th' castle, for my writ[135]
    Is on the life of Lear and on Cordelia.
    Nay, send in time.
Albany   Run, run, O, run!
Edgar   To who, my lord? Who hath the office? (*to Edmund*)
    Send
    Thy token of reprieve.
Edmund   Well thought on, take my sword,   225
    Give it the[136] captain.
Edgar   (*to Attendant*) Haste thee, for thy life.

EXIT ATTENDANT

Edmund He hath commission[137] from thy wife and me
    To hang Cordelia in the prison, and
    To lay the blame upon her own despair,
    That she fordid[138] herself.   230
Albany   The gods defend her! Bear him hence awhile.

EDMUND CARRIED OFF

ENTER LEAR, WITH CORDELIA DEAD IN HIS ARMS,
EDGAR, CAPTAIN, AND OTHERS FOLLOWING

Lear   Howl, howl, howl! O you are men of[139] stones.
    Had I your tongues and eyes, I'ld use them so

134 despite of = scorning, defying
135 written command
136 to the
137 orders, instructions
138 killed
139 made of

That heaven's vault should crack. She's gone for ever.

235   I know when one is dead, and when one lives,

She's dead as earth. (*setting her down*) Lend me a looking-glass,

If that her breath will mist or stain the stone,

Why then she lives.

Kent   Is this the promised end?[140]

Edgar   Or image[141] of that horror?

Albany   Fall, and cease![142]

240 *Lear*   This feather stirs, she lives! If it be so,

It is a chance[143] which does redeem all sorrows

That ever I have felt.

Kent   O my good master!

Lear   Prithee, away.

Edgar   'Tis noble Kent, your friend.

Lear   A plague upon you, murderers, traitors all!

245   I might have saved her, now she's gone for ever!

Cordelia, Cordelia, stay a little. Ha!

What is't thou say'st? Her voice was ever soft,

Gentle, and low, an excellent thing in woman.

I killed the slave that was a-hanging thee.

Captain 'Tis true, my lords, he did.

250 *Lear*   Did I not, fellow?

I have seen the day, with my good biting falchion[144]

I would have made them skip.[145] I am old now,

---

140 i.e., the end of everything: Judgment Day, the Day of Doom

141 the image / representation

142 fall, and cease = let the skies / heavens fall, and everything end

143 (1) fortune, luck, (2) opportunity, (3) event, happening

144 biting falchion = sharp, curved broadsword (FOALshin)

145 (1) hop about, (2) run away

And these same crosses spoil[146] me. Who are you?

Mine eyes are not o' the best, I'll tell you straight.

Kent   If Fortune brag of two she loved and hated,   255

One of them we behold.

Lear   This is a dull sight.[147] Are you not Kent?

Kent   The same,

Your servant Kent. Where is your servant Caius?

Lear   He's a good fellow, I can tell you that.

He'll strike, and quickly too. He's dead and rotten.   260

Kent   No my good lord, I am the very[148] man.

Lear   I'll see that straight.[149]

Kent   That, from your first of difference[150] and decay,

Have followed your sad steps.

Lear   You are welcome hither.

Kent   Nor no man else.[151] All's cheerless, dark, and deadly.   265

Your eldest daughters have fordone themselves,

And desperately[152] are dead.

Lear   Ay, so I think.

Albany   He knows not what he says, and vain it is

That we present us to him.

Edgar   Very bootless.[153]

ENTER CAPTAIN

146 crosses spoil = afflictions/troubles/misfortunes plunder/rob

147 (1) my eyes are not keen, *or* (2) Cordelia's body is a gloomy/melancholy/
    depressing sight

148 same

149 in good time

150 change, alteration

151 (1) that's exactly who I am, (2) neither me nor anyone else

152 in despair/hopelessness

153 useless

Captain (*to Albany*) Edmund is dead, my lord.

270 *Albany*   That's but a trifle

here.

You lords and noble friends, know our intent.

What comfort to this great decay[154] may come

Shall be applied. For us[155] we will resign,

During the life of this old majesty,

275 To him our absolute power (*to Edgar and Kent*), you[156] to

your rights,

With boot,[157] and such addition as your honors

Have more than merited. All friends shall taste

The wages of their virtue, and all foes

The cup of their deservings. O see, see!

280 *Lear*   And my poor fool[158] is hanged! No, no, no life!

Why should a dog, a horse, a rat, have life,

And thou no breath at all? Thou'lt come no more,

Never, never, never, never, never!

Pray you, undo this button.[159] Thank you, sir.

285 Do you see this? Look on her, look, her lips,

Look there, look there!

LEAR DIES

Edgar   He faints, my lord, my lord!

Kent   Break, heart, I prithee, break.

Edgar   (*to Lear*) Look up, my lord.

---

154 decline, in Lear

155 as for me

156 and you

157 gain, profit, compensation

158 Cordelia (fool = term of endearment)

159 i.e., Lear feels himself suffocating

Kent   Vex not his ghost, O let him pass. He hates him,
        That would upon the rack[160] of this tough[161] world
        Stretch him out longer.

Edgar   He is gone indeed.   290

Kent   The wonder is, he hath endured so long,
        He but usurped[162] his life.

Albany Bear them from hence. Our present business
        Is general woe. (*to Kent and Edgar*) Friends of my soul, you
        twain
        Rule in this realm, and the gored[163] state sustain.   295

Kent   I have a journey, sir, shortly to go.
        My master[164] calls me, I must not say no.

Edgar   The weight of this sad time we must obey;
        Speak what we feel, not what we ought to say.
        The oldest hath borne most, we that are young   300
        Shall never see so much, nor live so long.

EXEUNT, WITH A DEAD MARCH[165]

160 instrument of torture
161 (1) severe, painful, (2) sturdy, strong
162 but usurped = only assumed/bore
163 pierced, stabbed
164 Lear? God?
165 dead march = slow funeral music

AN ESSAY BY HAROLD BLOOM

I n the long reaction against A. C. Bradley's *Shakespearean Tragedy* and *Oxford Lectures on Poetry,* we have been warned endlessly against meditating upon the girlhood of Shakespeare's heroines or brooding upon the earlier marital days of the Macbeths. Yet Shakespearean representation, as the critic A. D. Nuttall observes, allows us to see aspects of reality we would not otherwise recognize. I would go beyond Nuttall to suggest that Shakespeare has molded both our sense of reality and our cognitive modes of apprehending that reality to a far greater degree than Homer or Plato, Montaigne or Nietzsche, Freud or Proust. Only the Bible rivals Shakespeare as an influence upon our sense of how human character, thinking, personality ought to be imitated through, in, or by language. No Western writer shows less consciousness of belatedness than Shakespeare, yet his true precursor is not Marlowe but the Bible. *King Lear* as tragedy finds its only worthy forerunner in the Book of Job, to which John Holloway and Frank Kermode have compared it.

A comparison between the sufferings of Job and of Lear is likely to lead to some startling conclusions about the preternatural persuasiveness of Shakespearean representation, being as it is an art whose limits we have yet to discover. This art convinces us that Lear exposed to the storm, out on the heath, is a designedly Jobean figure. To be thrown from being king of Britain to a fugitive in the open, pelted by merciless weather, and betrayed by ungrateful daughters is indeed an unpleasant fate, but is it truly Jobean? Job, after all, has experienced an even more dreadful sublimity; his son, daughters, servants, sheep, camels, and houses all have been destroyed by Satanic fires, and his direct, physical torment far transcends Lear's, not to mention that he still suffers his wife, while we never do hear anything about Lear's queen, who amazingly brought forth monsters of the deep in Goneril and Regan, but also Cordelia, a soul in bliss. What would Lear's wife have said, had she accompanied her royal husband onto the heath?

> So went Satan forth from the presence of the LORD, and
> smote Job with sore boils from the sole of his foot unto
> his crown.
>
> And he took him a potsherd to scrape himself withal;
> and he sat down among the ashes.
>
> Then said his wife unto him, Dost thou still retain
> thine integrity? curse God, and die.

That Shakespeare intended his audience to see Job as the model for Lear's situation (though hardly for Lear himself) seems likely, on the basis of a pattern of allusions in the drama. An imagery that associates humans with worms, and with dust, is strikingly present in both works. Lear himself presumably thinks of Job when he desperately asserts, "I will be the pattern of all patience" (3.2.35), a dreadful irony considering the king's ferociously impatient nature. Job is the righteous man handed over to the Accuser, but Lear is a blind king, who knows neither himself nor his daughters. Though Lear suffers the storm's fury, he is not Job-like either in his earlier sufferings (which he greatly magnifies) or in his relationship to the divine. It is another indication of Shakespeare's strong originality that he persuades us of the Jobean dignity and grandeur of Lear's first sufferings, even though to a considerable degree they are brought about by Lear himself, in sharp contrast to Job's absolute blamelessness. When Lear says that he is a man more sinned against than sinning, we tend to believe him, but is this really true at that point?

Only proleptically, as a prophesy, but again this is Shakespeare's astonishing originality, founded upon the representation of *impending change,* a change to be worked within Lear by his own listening to, and reflecting upon, what he himself speaks aloud in his increasing fury. He goes into the storm scene on the heath still screaming in anger, goes mad with that anger, and comes out of the storm with crucial change deeply in process within him, full of paternal love for the Fool and of concern for the supposed madman, Edgar impersonating Poor Tom. Lear's constant changes from then until the terrible end remain the most remarkable instance of a representation of a human transformation anywhere in imaginative literature.

But why did Shakespeare risk the paradigm of Job, since Lear, early and late, is so unlike Job, and since the play is anything but a theodicy? Milton remarked that the Book of Job was the rightful model for a "brief epic," such as his *Paradise Regained,* but in what sense can it be an appropriate model for a tragedy? Shakespeare may have been pondering his setting of *King Lear* in a Britain seven centuries before the time of Christ, a placement historically earlier than he attempted anywhere else, except for the Trojan War of *Troilus and Cressida. Lear* presumably is not a Christian play, though Cordelia is an eminently Christian personage, who says that she is about her father's business, in an overt allusion to the Gospel of Luke. But the Christian God and Jesus Christ are not relevant to the cosmos of *King Lear*. So appalling is the tragedy of this tragedy that Shakespeare shrewdly sets it before the Christian dispensation, in what he may have intuited was the time of Job. If *Macbeth* is Shakespeare's one full-scale venture into a Gnostic cosmos (and I think it was), then *King Lear* risks a more complete and catastrophic tragedy than anything in the genre before or since.

Job, rather oddly, ultimately receives the reward of his virtue; but Lear, purified and elevated, suffers instead the horror of Cordelia's murder by the underlings of Edmund. I think then that Shakespeare invoked the Book of Job in order to emphasize the absolute negativity of Lear's tragedy. Had Lear's wife been alive, she would have done well to emulate Job's wife, so as to advise her husband to curse God and die. Pragmatically, it would have been a better fate than the one Lear finally suffers in the play.

The Gloucester subplot may be said to work deliberately against Lear's Jobean sense of his own uniqueness as a sufferer; his tragedy will not be the one he desires, for it is not so much a tragedy of filial ingratitude as of a kind of apocalyptic nihilism, universal in its implications. We do not sympathize with Lear's immense curses, though they are increasingly related to his rising fear of madness, which is also his fear of a womanly nature rising up within him. Finally Lear's madness, like his curses, proceeds from his biblical sense of himself; desiring to be everything in himself, he fears greatly that he is nothing in himself. His obsession with his own blindness seems related to an aging vitalist's fear of impotence and so of mortality. Yet Lear is not just any old hero, nor even just a great king falling away into madness and death. Shakespeare allows him a diction more preternaturally eloquent than is spoken by anyone else in this or any other drama, and that evidently never will be matched again. Lear matters because his language is uniquely strong, and because we are persuaded that this splendor is wholly appropriate to him.

We can remark, following Nietzsche and Freud, that only one Western image participates neither in origin nor in end: the image of the father. Lear, more than Gloucester, more than any other figure even in Shakespeare, is *the* image of the father, the metaphor of paternal authority. Nature, in the drama, is both origin and end, mother and catastrophe, and it ought to be Lear's function to hold and safeguard the middle ground between the daemonic world and the realm of the gods. He fails, massively, and the ensuing tragedy engulfs an entire world, with a poignance unmatched in literature:

Edgar   But who comes here?

ENTER KING LEAR, FANTASTICALLY ADORNED
WITH WILDFLOWERS

    The safer sense will ne'er accommodate
    His master thus.

Lear   No, they cannot touch me for crying. I am the King himself.

Edgar O thou side-piercing sight!

Lear   Nature's above art in that respect. There's your press-money. That fellow handles his bow like a crow-keeper. Draw me a clothier's yard. Look, look, a mouse! Peace, peace, this

piece of toasted cheese will do 't. There's my gauntlet, I'll
prove it on a giant. Bring up the brown bills. O well flown,
bird! I' the clout, i' the clout. Hewgh! Give the word.

Edgar   Sweet marjoram.

Lear   Pass.

Gloucester I know that voice.

Lear   Ha! Goneril with a white beard? They flattered me
like a dog, and told me I had the white hairs in my beard, ere
the black ones were there. To say "ay" and "no" to everything
that I said. "Ay," and "no" too, was no good divinity. When
the rain came to wet me once, and the wind to make me
chatter, when the thunder would not peace at my bidding,
there I found 'em, there I smelt 'em out. Go to, they are not
men o' their words, they told me I was everything. 'Tis a lie, I
am not ague-proof.

Gloucester The trick of that voice I do well remember:
     Is 't not the King?

Lear   Ay, every inch a king.
When I do stare, see how the subject quakes.
I pardon that man's life. What was thy cause?
Adultery?
Thou shalt not die. Die for adultery? No,
The wren goes to 't, and the small gilded fly
Does lecher in my sight.
Let copulation thrive, for Gloucester's bastard son
Was kinder to his father than my daughters
Got 'tween the lawful sheets.
To 't, luxury, pell-mell, for I lack soldiers.
Behold yond simpering dame,
Whose face between her forks presages snow,

That minces virtue, and does shake the head
To hear of pleasure's name.
The fitchew, nor the soilèd horse, goes to 't
With a more riotous appetite.
Down from the waist they are centaurs,
Though women all above.
But to the girdle do the gods inherit,
Beneath is all the fiends'.
There's hell, there's darkness, there is the sulphurous pit,
Burning, scalding, stench, consumption.
Fie, fie, fie! Pah, pah!
Give me an ounce of civet,
Good apothecary, to sweeten my imagination.
There's money for thee.

Gloucester   O, let me kiss that hand!

Lear   Let me wipe it first, it smells of mortality.

Gloucester O ruined piece of nature! This great world
Shall so wear out to nought. Dost thou know me?

Lear   I remember thine eyes well enough. Dost thou squiny
at me? No, do thy worst, blind Cupid, I'll not love. Read thou
this challenge, mark but the penning of it.

Gloucester Were all the letters suns, I could not see one.

Edgar   (*aside*) I would not take this from report. It is,
And my heart breaks at it.

Lear   Read.

Gloucester What, with the case of eyes?

Lear   O ho, are you there with me? No eyes in your head,
nor no money in your purse? Your eyes are in a heavy case,
your purse in a light, yet you see how this world goes.

Gloucester I see it feelingly.

Lear   What, art mad? A man may see how this world goes
with no eyes. Look with thine eyes. See how yond justice rails
upon yond simple thief. Hark in thine ear. Change places
and, handy-dandy, which is the justice, which is the thief?
Thou hast seen a farmer's dog bark at a beggar?

Gloucester Ay, sir.

Lear   And the creature run from the cur? There thou
mightst behold the great image of authority: a dog's obeyed
in office.

Thou rascal beadle, hold thy bloody hand!

Why dost thou lash that whore? Strip thine own back.

Thou hotly lusts to use her in that kind

For which thou whipp'st her. The usurer hangs the cozener.

Through tattered clothes small vices do appear.

Robes and furred gowns hide all. Plate sin with gold,

And the strong lance of justice hurtless breaks.

Arm it in rags, a pigmy's straw does pierce it.

None does offend, none, I say, none, I'll able 'em.

Take that of me, my friend, who have the power

To seal th' accuser's lips. Get thee glass eyes,

And like a scurvy politican, seem

To see the things thou dost not. Now, now, now, now.

Pull off my boots. Harder, harder. So.

Edgar   O matter and impertinency mixed,
Reason in madness!

Lear   If thou wilt weep my fortunes, take my eyes.

I know thee well enough, thy name is Gloucester.

Thou must be patient, we came crying hither.

Thou know'st, the first time that we smell the air,

We wawl and cry. I will preach to thee. Mark.

Gloucester Alack, alack the day!
Lear When we are born, we cry that we are come
   To this great stage of fools.

[4.6.80–181]

Frank Kermode justly remarks of this scene that it is at once Shakespeare's boldest effort of imagination and utterly lacking in merely *narrative* function. Indeed, it strictly lacks all function, and the tragedy does not need it. We do not reason the need: poetic language never has gone further. Edgar, who once pretended madness, begins by observing that "the safer sense" or sane mind cannot accommodate itself to the vision of the ultimate paternal authority having gone mad. But "safer sense" here also refers to seeing, and the entire scene is a vastation organized about the dual images of eyesight and of fatherhood, images linked yet also severed throughout the play. The sight that pierces Edgar's side is intolerable to a quiet hero whose only quest has been to preserve the image of his father's authority. His father, blinded Gloucester, recognizing authority by its voice, laments the mad king as nature's ruined masterpiece and prophesies that a similar madness will wear away the entire world into nothingness. The prophecy will be fulfilled in the drama's closing scene, but is deferred so that the reign of "reason in madness" or sight in blindness can be continued. Pathos transcends all limits in Lear's great and momentary breakthrough into sanity, as it cries out to Gloucester, and to all of us, "If thou wilt weep my fortunes, take my eyes."

Hardly the pattern of all patience, Lear nevertheless has earned the convincing intensity of telling Gloucester, "Thou must be patient." What follows however is not Jobean but Shakespearean, perhaps even the essence of the drama's prophecy: "we came crying hither" and "When we are born, we cry that we are come / To this great stage of fools." The great theatrical trope encompasses every meaning the play crams into the word "fool": actor, moral being, idealist, child, dear one, madman, victim, truth-teller. As Northrop Frye observes, the only characters in *King Lear* who are not fools are Edmund, Goneril, Regan, Cornwall, and their followers.

Lear's own Fool undergoes a subtle transformation as the drama burns on, from an oracle of forbidden wisdom to a frightened child, until at last he simply disappears, as though he blent into the identity of the dead Cordelia when the broken Lear cries out, "And my poor fool is hanged!" (5.3.280). Subtler still is the astonishing transformation of the most interesting consciousness in the play, the bastard Edmund, Shakespeare's most intensely theatrical villain, surpassing even Richard III and Iago. Edmund, as theatrical as Barabas, Marlowe's Jew of Malta, might almost be a sly portrait of Christopher Marlowe himself. As the purest and coolest Machiavel in stage history, at least until he knows he has received his death-wound, Edmund is both a remarkably antic and charming Satan, and a being with real self-knowledge, which makes him particularly dangerous in a world presided over by Lear, who "hath ever but slenderly known himself" (1.1.293–94), as Regan remarks.

Edmund's mysterious and belated metamorphosis as the play nears its end, a movement from playing oneself to being oneself, turns upon his complex reactions to his own deathly musing: "Yet Edmund was beloved (5.3.216). It is peculiarly shocking and pathetic that his lovers were Goneril and Regan, monsters who proved their love by suicide and murder, or by victimage, but

Shakespeare seems to have wished to give us a virtuoso display of his original art in changing character through the representation of a growing inwardness. Outrageously refreshing at his most evil (Edgar is a virtuous bore in contrast to him), Edmund is the most attractive of Jacobean hero-villains and inevitably captures both Goneril and Regan, evidently with singularly little effort. His dangerous attractiveness is one of the principal unexplored clues to the enigmas of Shakespeare's most sublime achievement. That Edmund has gusto, an exuberance befitting his role as natural son, is merely part of the given. His intelligence and will are more central to him, and darken the meanings of *King Lear*.

Wounded to death by Edgar, his brother, Edmund yields to fortune: "The wheel is come full circle, I am here" (5.3.168). Where he is not is upon Lear's "wheel of fire," in a place of saving madness. Not only do Edmund and Lear exchange not a single word in the course of this vast drama, but it defies imagination to conceive of what they could say to one another. It is not only the intricacies of the double plot that keep Edmund and Lear apart; they have no language in common. Frye points out that "nature" takes on antithetical meanings in regard to the other, in Lear and Edmund, and this can be expanded to the realization that Lear, despite all his faults, is incapable of guile, but Edmund is incapable of an honest passion of any kind. The lover of both Goneril and Regan, he is passive towards both, and is moved by their deaths only to reflect upon what was for him the extraordinary reality that anyone, however monstrous, ever should have loved him at all.

Why does he reform, however belatedly and ineffectually, since Cordelia is murdered anyway; what are we to make of his final turn towards the light? Edmund's first reaction towards the news of the deaths of Goneril and Regan is the grimly dispassionate, "I was contracted to them both, all three / Now marry in an instant" (5.3.205–6), which identifies dying and marrying as a single act. In the actual moment of repentance, Edmund desperately says, "I pant for life. Some good I mean to do, / Despite of mine own nature" (219–20). This is not to say that nature no longer is his goddess, but rather than he is finally touched by images of connection or concern, be they as far apart as Edgar's care for Gloucester, or Goneril's and Regan's fiercely competitive lust for his own person.

I conclude by returning to my fanciful speculation that the Faustian Edmund is not only overtly Marlovian, but indeed may be Shakespeare's charmed but wary portrait of elements in Christopher Marlowe himself. Edmund represents the way not to go, and yet is the only figure in *King Lear* who is truly at home in its apocalyptic cosmos. The wheel comes full circle for him, but he has limned his nightpiece, and it was his best.

FURTHER READING

This is not a bibliography but a selective set of starting places.

Texts

Shakespeare, William. *The First Folio of Shakespeare,* 2d ed. Edited by
  Charlton Hinman. Introduction by Peter W. M. Blayney. New York:
  W. W. Norton, 1996.
———. *King Lear: The Quarto of 1608.* Shakespeare Quarto Facsimiles,
  1. Oxford: Clarendon Press, 1939.
———. *King Lear: The New Variorum Edition.* Edited by Horace
  Howard Furness. Philadelphia: Lippincott, 1908.
Urkowitz, Steven. *Shakespeare's Revision of "King Lear."* Princteon, N.J.:
  Princeton University Press, 1980.

Language

Dobson, E. J. *English Pronunciation, 1500–1700.* 2d ed. Oxford: Oxford
  University Press, 1968.
Houston, John Porter. *The Rhetoric of Poetry in the Renaissance and
  Seventeenth Century.* Baton Rouge: Louisiana State University Press,
  1983.
———. *Shakespearean Sentences: A Study in Style and Syntax.* Baton
  Rouge: Louisiana State University Press, 1988.
Kermode, Frank. *Shakespeare's Language.* New York: Farrar, Straus and
  Giroux, 2000.

Kökeritz, Helge. *Shakespeare's Pronunciation.* New Haven: Yale University Press, 1953.

Lanham, Richard A. *The Motives of Eloquence: Literary Rhetoric in the Renaissance.* New Haven and London: Yale University Press, 1976.

The Oxford English Dictionary: Second Edition on CD-ROM, version 3.0. New York: Oxford University Press, 2002.

Raffel, Burton. *From Stress to Stress: An Autobiography of English Prosody.* Hamden, Conn.: Archon Books, 1992.

Ronberg, Gert. *A Way with Words: The Language of English Renaissance Literature.* London: Arnold, 1992.

Trousdale, Marion. *Shakespeare and the Rhetoricians.* Chapel Hill: University of North Carolina Press, 1982.

Culture

Bindoff, S. T. *Tudor England.* Baltimore: Penguin, 1950.

Bradbrook, M. C. *Shakespeare: The Poet in His World.* New York: Columbia University Press, 1978.

Brown, Cedric C., ed. *Patronage, Politics, and Literary Tradition in England, 1558–1658.* Detroit, Mich.: Wayne State University Press, 1993.

Bush, Douglas. *Prefaces to Renaissance Literature.* New York: W. W. Norton, 1965.

Buxton, John. *Elizabethan Taste.* London: Harvester, 1963.

Cowan, Alexander. *Urban Europe, 1500–1700.* New York: Oxford University Press, 1998.

Driver, Tom E. *The Sense of History in Greek and Shakespearean Drama.* New York: Columbia University Press, 1960.

Finucci, Valeria, and Regina Schwartz, eds. *Desire in the Renaissance: Psychoanalysis and Literature.* Princeton, N.J.: Princeton University Press, 1994.

Fumerton, Patricia, and Simon Hunt, eds. *Renaissance Culture and the Everyday.* Philadelphia: University of Pennsylvania Press, 1999.

Halliday, F. E. *Shakespeare in His Age.* South Brunswick, N.J.: Yoseloff, 1965.

Harrison, G. B., ed. *The Elizabethan Journals: Being a Record of Those*

Things Most Talked of During the Years 1591–1597. Abridged ed. 2 vols. New York: Doubleday Anchor, 1965.

Harrison, William. *The Description of England: The Classic Contemporary [1577] Account of Tudor Social Life.* Edited by Georges Edelen. Washington, D.C.: Folger Shakespeare Library, 1968. Reprint, New York: Dover, 1994.

Jardine, Lisa. "Introduction." In Jardine, *Reading Shakespeare Historically.* London: Routledge, 1996.

———. *Worldly Goods: A New History of the Renaissance.* London: Macmillan, 1996.

Jeanneret, Michel. *A Feast of Words: Banquets and Table Talk in the Renaissance.* Translated by Jeremy Whiteley and Emma Hughes. Chicago: University of Chicago Press, 1991.

Kernan, Alvin. *Shakespeare, the King's Playwright: Theater in the Stuart Court, 1603–1613.* New Haven and London: Yale University Press, 1995.

Lockyer, Roger. *Tudor and Stuart Britain, 1471–1714.* London: Longmans, 1964.

Norwich, John Julius. *Shakespeare's Kings: The Great Plays and the History of England in the Middle Ages, 1337–1485.* New York: Scribner, 2000.

Rose, Mary Beth, ed. *Renaissance Drama as Cultural History: Essays from Renaissance Drama, 1977–1987.* Evanston, Ill.: Northwestern University Press, 1990.

Schmidgall, Gary. *Shakespeare and the Courtly Aesthetic.* Berkeley: University of California Press, 1981.

Smith, G. Gergory, ed. *Elizabethan Critical Essays.* 2 vols. Oxford: Clarendon Press, 1904.

Tillyard, E. M. W. *The Elizabethan World Picture.* London: Chatto and Windus, 1943. Reprint, Harmondsworth: Penguin, 1963.

Willey, Basil. *The Seventeenth Century Background: Studies in the Thought of the Age in Relation to Poetry and Religion.* New York: Columbia University Press, 1933. Reprint, New York: Doubleday, 1955.

Wilson, F. P. *The Plague in Shakespeare's London.* 2d ed. Oxford: Oxford University Press, 1963.

Wilson, John Dover. *Life in Shakespeare's England: A Book of Elizabethan*

Prose. 2d ed. Cambridge: Cambridge University Press, 1913. Reprint, Harmondsworth: Penguin, 1944.

Zimmerman, Susan, and Ronald F. E. Weissman, eds. *Urban Life in the Renaissance.* Newark: University of Delaware Press, 1989.

Dramatic Development

Cohen, Walter. *Drama of a Nation: Public Theater in Renaissance England and Spain.* Ithaca, N.Y.: Cornell University Press, 1985.

Dessen, Alan C. *Shakespeare and the Late Moral Plays.* Lincoln: University of Nebraska Press, 1986.

Fraser, Russell A., and Norman Rabkin, eds. *Drama of the English Renaissance.* 2 vols. Upper Saddle River, N.J.: Prentice Hall, 1976.

Happé, Peter, ed. *Tudor Interludes.* Harmondsworth: Penguin, 1972.

Laroque, François. *Shakespeare's Festive World: Elizabethan Seasonal Entertainment and the Professional Stage.* Translated by Janet Lloyd. Cambridge: Cambridge University Press, 1991.

Norland, Howard B. *Drama in Early Tudor Britain, 1485–1558.* Lincoln: University of Nebraska Press, 1995.

Theater and Stage

Doran, Madeleine. *Endeavors of Art: A Study of Form in Elizabethan Drama.* Milwaukee: University of Wisconsin Press, 1954.

Grene, David. *The Actor in History: Studies in Shakespearean Stage Poetry.* University Park: Pennsylvania State University Press, 1988.

Gurr, Andrew. *Playgoing in Shakespeare's London.* Cambridge: Cambridge University Press, 1987.

———. *The Shakespearian Stage, 1574–1642.* 3d ed. Cambridge: Cambridge University Press, 1992.

Halliday, F. E. *A Shakespeare Companion, 1564–1964.* Rev. ed. Harmondsworth: Penguin, 1964.

Harrison, G. B. *Elizabethan Plays and Players.* Ann Arbor: University of Michigan Press, 1956.

Holmes, Martin. *Shakespeare and His Players.* New York: Scribner, 1972.

Ingram, William. *The Business of Playing: The Beginnings of the Adult*

Professional Theater in Elizabethan London. Ithaca, N.Y.: Cornell University Press, 1992.

Lamb, Charles. *The Complete Works and Letters of Charles Lamb.* Edited by Saxe Commins. New York: Modern Library, 1935.

LeWinter, Oswald, ed. *Shakespeare in Europe.* Cleveland, Ohio: Meridian, 1963.

Marcus, Leah S. *Unediting the Renaissance: Shakespeare, Marlowe, Milton.* London: Routledge, 1996.

Orgel, Stephen. *The Authentic Shakespeare, and Other Problems of the Early Modern Stage.* New York: Routledge, 2002.

Salgado, Gamini. *Eyewitnesses of Shakespeare: First Hand Accounts of Performances, 1590–1890.* New York: Barnes and Noble, 1975.

Stern, Tiffany. *Rehearsal from Shakespeare to Sheridan.* Oxford: Clarendon Press, 2000.

Thomson, Peter. *Shakespeare's Professional Career.* Cambridge: Cambridge University Press, 1992.

Webster, Margaret. *Shakespeare without Tears.* New York: Whittlesey House, 1942.

Weimann, Robert. *Shakespeare and the Popular Tradition in the Theater: Studies in the Social Dimension of Dramatic Form and Function.* Edited by Robert Schwartz. Baltimore: Johns Hopkins University Press, 1978.

Wikander, Matthew H. *The Play of Truth and State: Historical Drama from Shakespeare to Brecht.* Baltimore: Johns Hopkins University Press, 1986.

Yachnin, Paul. *Stage-Wrights: Shakespeare, Jonson, Middleton, and the Making of Theatrical Value.* Philadelphia: University of Pennsylvania Press, 1997.

Biography

Halliday, F. E. *The Life of Shakespeare.* Rev. ed. London: Duckworth, 1964.

Honigmann, F. A. J. *Shakespeare: The "Lost Years."* 2d ed. Manchester: Manchester University Press, 1998.

Schoenbaum, Samuel. *Shakespeare's Lives.* New ed. Oxford: Clarendon Press, 1991.

———. *William Shakespeare: A Compact Documentary Life.* Oxford: Oxford University Press, 1977.

General

Bergeron, David M., and Geraldo U. de Sousa. *Shakespeare: A Study and Research Guide.* 3d ed. Lawrence: University of Kansas Press, 1995.

Berryman, John. *Berryman's Shakespeare.* Edited by John Haffenden. Preface by Robert Giroux. New York: Farrar, Straus and Giroux, 1999.

Bradby, Anne, ed. *Shakespearian Criticism, 1919–35.* London: Oxford University Press, 1936.

Colie, Rosalie L. *Shakespeare's Living Art.* Princeton, N.J.: Princeton University Press, 1974.

Dean, Leonard F., ed. *Shakespeare: Modern Essays in Criticism.* Rev. ed. New York: Oxford University Press, 1967.

Goddard, Harold C. *The Meaning of Shakespeare.* 2 vols. Chicago: University of Chicago Press, 1951.

Kaufmann, Ralph J. *Elizabethan Drama: Modern Essays in Criticism.* New York: Oxford University Press, 1961.

McDonald, Russ. *The Bedford Companion to Shakespeare: An Introduction with Documents.* Boston: Bedford, 1996.

Raffel, Burton. *How to Read a Poem.* New York: Meridian, 1984.

Ricks, Christopher, ed. *English Drama to 1710.* Rev. ed. Harmondsworth: Sphere, 1987.

Siegel, Paul N., ed. *His Infinite Variety: Major Shakespearean Criticism Since Johnson.* Philadelphia: Lippincott, 1964.

Sweeting, Elizabeth J. *Early Tudor Criticism: Linguistic and Literary.* Oxford: Blackwell, 1940.

Van Doren, Mark. *Shakespeare.* New York: Holt, 1939.

Weiss, Theodore. *The Breath of Clowns and Kings: Shakespeare's Early Comedies and Histories.* New York: Atheneum, 1971.

Wells, Stanley, ed. *The Cambridge Companion to Shakespeare Studies,* Cambridge: Cambridge University Press, 1986.

FINDING LIST

Repeated unfamiliar words and meanings, alphabetically arranged, with act, scene, and footnote number of first occurrence, in the spelling (form) of that first occurrence